I Am Coming Home

Remember the
" Vets ! "

Gwen J. Mc Garry

I AM COMING HOME

———

A True Story of Survival in WWII Japanese Prison Camps

Wendell Hickman McGarry, DDS

As told to Gwen J. McGarry

———

Cover Painting by Wesley R. Jacobson

Southern Utah University Press
Cedar City, Utah
2012

First published in 2013
by Southern Utah University Press
Cedar City, Utah
Copyright © Gwen J. McGarry, 2013
ISBN 978-0-93-561538-8
LCCN 2012953921
Designed and typeset by Maggie Hyde and Sheri Butler
Printed in the United States by Lightning Source

*To all the POWs who lived though hell,
who survived to more deeply appreciate and
love the United States of America
and the freedom she represents.*

TABLE OF CONTENTS

ACKNOWLEDGMENTS

My special thanks to those who gave assistance in many ways as I struggled to record this segment of Wendell's story. To his good Manti friends and neighbors Don Tibbs and Don Simmons, both WWII Vets, who read the manuscript and provided valuable emotional insight. To his 92 year old sister LaRue McGarry Brewster—Wendell's only surviving sibling— my special appreciation for her loving comments when she read the manuscript. To my dear educator friends, Marie Beacham and Ardith Peterson for reading and offering candid comments. To David Rosier, English Professor at Snow College, who read, evaluated and corrected the mechanics of the story. To Brenton Yorgason, distinguished author of more than one hundred volumes, who encouraged and made me believe the manuscript could evolve into an honest-to-goodness book. To Shirley Bahlmann, author and lover of Sanpete County pioneer history, who was at my beck and call, who generously shared her personal experience, suggestions and expertise in writing and computer formatting, whose loving encouragement filled my energy tank many times, pushing the project to completion. To Ben Steele, renowned Montana artist, XPOW and dear friend of Wendell's and mine for generously permitting the inclusion of his graphic prison camp-life sketch. To Ben's wife, Shirley Steele, poet and treasured friend, for her kind expressions and expert literary advice. To Professor Ralph Brenchley, amazing Snow College history teacher and retired National Guard Colonel and his wife Clarene, elementary teacher extraordinaire, who read and offered suggestions. To former Manti Temple President and author Ed Pinegar, who when he read the manuscript remarked, "He was truly a hero." To former Governor Norman Bangerter for his kind remarks found on the back cover. For the love, encouragement, support, cajoling, and questioning of, "Is it finished yet?" by Wendell's children, my children, and by our forty-plus grandchildren. Last, but by no means least, to my dear friend Michael Benson, President of Southern Utah University for suggesting SUU as a possible publisher, to Professor Matt Nickerson and Dr. Larry Ping, Jonathan McNaughtan, and Matt Roan, both President's Council Fellows at SUU, and to Sheri Butler and the publishing staff for their expenditure of time and effort in getting the book actually printed, my undying gratitude.

And finally, to Grandson Welsey R. Jacobson for the painting of his Grandfather with his mother coming home, which graces the front cover, my very special thanks.

Gwen J. McGarry

INTRODUCTION

THE MAN BEHIND THE STORY
TO WAR AND HOME AGAIN

Wendell Hickman McGarry was born near Manderfield, Beaver County, Utah, June 9, 1918, the 5th child in Sheridan and Fern Hickman McGarry's family of nine children. Shortly after his birth they moved to Salt Lake City. No one could have guessed he would grow up to eventually become an army medic and serve in a war where he was captured by a ruthless enemy. Ironically, he was not the first McGarry to suffer this fate. His paternal grandfather, James McGarry, one of the Green Mountain Boys of Vermont, was captured in 1860 by southern rebels during the Civil War. Barely 17 years old, he survived 11 months of starvation, and disease in filthy conditions while incarcerated in the notorious Andersonville Prison. Paralleling his grandfather, Wendell endured nearly three brutal years in several World War II Japanese prison camps suffering the same adversity and pain; perhaps more.

In spite of this horrific experience, he was completely devoid of animosity toward the Japanese people as a race. In 1982 Eiichi, a Japanese Snow College, student asked the McGarrys to be his host family. Wendell replied, "Of course, he doesn't know any more about World War II than my kids." Eiichi was followed by two Japanese girls, Satomi and Aki. Wendell helped perfect their English language, he taught them American traditions, the joy of serving others, and the value of hard work. He nurtured in them Christian values, to pray in gratitude for every meal. He demonstrated love of family, loyalty and reverence for the United States of America. However, he admitted he had not totally forgiven those individuals who abused him as a POW, and he was adamant about never buying a Toyota vehicle.

Working his way through South High School and the University of Utah, his education was put on hold in 1941 when young men were drafted into the military. Choosing to enlist in the Army, he was shipped to the Philippine Islands nine months before a surge of patriotism awakened in the United States after the infamous Japanese attack on Pearl Harbor in the Hawaiian Islands. Captured on Corregidor Island in May 1942, Wendell was liberated at Bilibid Prison in February 1945. He died May 21, 2004 in the Sanpete Valley Hospital in Mt. Pleasant, Utah surrounded by his wife and family.

For 45 years, Wendell often voiced his reluctance to share. "I have no desire whatsoever to talk about, write, or even remember the experiences I had while a Japanese POW!" During that interval of time, he rarely spoke of the difficulties he endured in the Philippine Islands Prison Camps.

His resistance dissolved in 1990 when he met with fellow XPOWs at a Northwest Chapter of the American Defenders of Bataan and Corregidor reunion in Sand Point, Idaho. The turning point came when he realized he wasn't the only one who felt that way. Most of them were reluctant to re-live the horror of their prison camp days. One notable exception to verbalizing his experiences was Gene Jacobsen, a Bataan Death March survivor, who'd written of his wartime experiences in graphic detail. The other XPOWs were amazed at his ease in talking about his difficult challenges in prison camp. He became an inspiration, helping others to overcome their hesitancy to talk about the pain they endured through deprivation of independence and freedom, torture, starvation and loneliness.

Once the wall of resistance to remember melted away suppressed memories came pouring out like floods through a breached dam. These exceptional men bonded together and became passengers on the same vessel floating on a sea of emotions. A recollection of one person would invite the memory of another to be shared. And so it went for hours on end. They laughed, they cried together—they became brothers. Wendell was surprised to learn that the experiences of many

XPOWs who had been in the same place at the same time were remembered in a totally different way. As individuals they had been affected mentally, and sometimes physically, completely unlike anyone else.

At this same reunion, Wendell's deliberate mental and emotional blocks became vividly apparent when Walter Pancratz, a fellow army medic from the Malinta Tunnel Hospital, greeted him warmly. From the blank look on Wendell's face, it was obvious he had completely forgotten Walter. Even though they'd come home on the same ship after liberation and spent time together in San Francisco, it took several minutes of reminiscing before Wendell's memory was jarred. Then a friendship that began as young men under the very difficult circumstances of war became a source of close camaraderie in their senior years.

The experience at Sandpoint was a revelation that signaled a turning point in Wendell's attitude, desire, and willingness to talk about those dreadful years. He was compelled to share his experiences, along with his hatred for the enemy, the fear and hopelessness of captivity, and his joy at being released from bondage.

Amazed with the information he shared on the way home from Sandpoint, Wendell's wife quickly recorded what he revealed. She wrote on the back of envelopes, napkins, and scraps of paper found in her purse. Later on, when it became apparent this was not a temporary reaction on Wendell's part, she wised up and carried small notebooks in which she wrote in more detail. A single question or comment would release a surge of in-depth descriptions of hunger, illness, and beatings he had endured, along with the negative emotions and feelings he harbored. He told of friendships formed in the ranks of fellow soldiers—one or two with the enemy. He expressed his deep affection for the Philippine Islands and her people. He became willing to share his experiences with others as well, to friends, senior citizens, high schools assemblies, addressing audiences on Memorial and Veterans Day, and taping interviews for his grandchildren to use for school assignments.

There was a definite feeling of relief after releasing the tide of pent-up emotions, fears, and experiences that were his unwelcome companions for so long. He was more relaxed in discussing past events with his family and friends. Verbal therapy worked in his favor. However, there was a limit on how long he would talk and how much he would say. When one of his best friends, Don Tibbs, a persuasive Utah District Court Judge, coaxed him into doing a video recording of his POW experience, the interview ended abruptly when Wendell stood up from his chair with, "That's enough!" and walked away from the still-running camera. That DVD is priceless because it's very much like Wendell and the way he did things.

The final decision to write this book was made after attending the concluding event at an ADBC (American Defenders of Bataan and Corregidor) reunion in 1994 at Cottage Grove, Oregon. At the Saturday night dinner, the Commander told of taking his ill wife into the emergency room at the local hospital and mentioning his military reunion to the young physician. With a puzzled look on his face, the doctor replied, "I know what a baton is, but what in the world is a Corregidor?"

A gasp of astonishment rippled through the audience as we realized this university educated young man knew nothing of significant events of World War II. Had he never been taught about it in school? Had he never known anyone who lived it or even cared about that time in history? That's when Wendell agreed it was important to record his personal history. Future generations needed to learn and care about the terrible things perpetrated by greed, envy, and desire for wealth and power of the leaders of nations and the masses who blindly followed them. His own posterity needed to know how their soldier grandfather fit into the picture of war; his feelings, experiences and the aftermath of it all.

After learning of his war experiences it is understandable why Wendell never bought just one of anything. He always purchased two or more of paper products, cleaning supplies, and clothing items such as socks, shirts, and pairs of shoes. Canned goods were often bought in case lots. He repeatedly referred to plump, ripe bananas as "officer's bananas," and he unfailingly bought several more than he and his wife could possibly eat before they became too ripe. They made a lot of banana bread.

Wendell was blessed with supreme patience, especially with his wife, unless he thought they were going to be late. No matter where they went be it church, dinner parties, medical appointments or a meeting of any kind, they were always early, never just on time and certainly never late. Once they began the drive home, he was immovable in heading straight there with no unnecessary stops. The other wives of XPOWs shared remarkably similar stories about their husbands' behavioral quirks as well.

While recordingWendell's, Gwen gained insight into the exquisite pain and suffering his parents were enduring not knowing his fate. An excerpt from one of his mother's letters in the summer of 1943 reads:

> My Dear Boy:
>
> I am so anxious to hear from you. All of my letters have been returned and I have not heard from you since you wrote the 19th of February, (1942). You have been gone over a year. Your birthday has come and gone and I have not been able to send you any greetings. I think of you every day and wonder where you are—Oh my dear, I hope you are not in any enemy camp. I cannot contain myself, if only I could get word to you some way. Only through God can I reach you, so I will have to be content until I hear from you.

One can only imagine the agonizingly bittersweet joy of his mother at receiving a postcard from Wendell in late 1943 written at Cabanatuan Prison Camp telling her that he was alive. Her letter dated September 1, 1943 states:

> My Dearest Wendell,
>
> We got your card stating that you were well. It was like a message from the great beyond. After nearly two years of silence, we were so overjoyed, you will never know how happy we were to learn you were well. I am hoping and praying this message will reach you in due time, that your heart may be gladdened as ours was.

The anguish of his parents would have increased immensely had they known of the physical, spiritual, and emotional abuse their son was enduring. To have been aware of his incessant hunger would have been heart wrenching.

The only written accounts of Wendell's prison experiences come from brief notes he made in a small Bible his mother gave him when he went into the Army and the letters he wrote from Corregidor before his capture. Sixty-plus years after the fact is a long time to rely on one's memory without benefit of the written word. Looking back on these experiences was often painful and disturbing for him. The passage of time and space tend to whitewash some things and to distort memories of the past. But Wendell did his best to record events with a degree of accuracy and portray his feelings after they came out of the closet of deliberate forgetting. It is hoped there will be patience on the part of the reader with the inadvertent errors or unintended omissions.

> From the beginning of the writing process his hope and mine has been to give his family a glimpse into these traumatic experiences, that they may take a virtual walk in his footsteps to better understand the deep seated feelings of their father and grandfather and the profound reverence for freedom he so fiercely guarded. Despite all her faults and imperfections the unconditional love he had for his country.
>
> In writing this story for Wendell, I have learned to appreciate more deeply the importance of home, family, country and the love of our Heavenly Father. I have sipped the cup of human kindness, of loyalty and friendship. I have tasted the bitterness of cruelty, misery and defeat. I have felt the hopelessness of captivity and the exaltation of freedom. I have witnessed the love and compassion of God.
>
> Gwen J. McGarry

– 1 –

CORREGIDOR BEFORE THE WAR

My future looked bright as a pre-med student at Salt Lake City's University of Utah in 1940-41, until the war clouds over Europe darkened the horizon of the United States. With them came the acceleration of the draft into the armed forces of all healthy young men eighteen years of age and older; single men being the first to be inducted.

Along with three of my high school friends, Frank Nesbitt, Jack Martin, and Herb Liester, who were engineering students, I decided to beat the draft and enlist in the Army. However, all three of them opted to wait until after their graduations in June. As I would not have graduated by then, I enlisted by myself.

On Thursday April 10, 1941, I raised my right hand to repeat the military oath administered to all of the new recruits at Fort Douglas Army Base in Salt Lake City which said:

> I do solemnly swear that I will support and defend the Constitution of the United States of America against all enemies, foreign or domestic, so help me God.

I had heard it before, but for the first time I wondered exactly what it would mean for me. I had been raised a city boy, having lived in the Salt Lake valley virtually all of my life, surrounded by the protection of the Wasatch Mountains in a typically safe, secure American environment. War was not a situation I had ever been seriously concerned about, but at that solemn moment, I wondered.

My orders stated I was to report almost immediately to the Presidio, a large army base near San Francisco where I was to be assigned to Ft. McDowell for a period of orientation. I would then be shipped to the Philippine Islands and serve in the Medical Detachment at Fort Mills, an American Army Base on Corregidor Island in Manila Bay. Although I was quite unaware of the strategic importance of this island to the United States, "Little did I know that these surroundings would become indelibly engraved on my mind forever." [1]

Immediately after the official induction into the Army, I boarded a bus with a number of other recruits and was driven directly to the Presidio. The first letter to my parents was written on April 12th. It said in part:

> We had a great trip to San Francisco. On arrival we went to the pier and boarded a ferry to Angel Island where Ft. McDowell is located. On the way there we passed Alcatraz prison. The first signs that we were really in the Army was the issuing of bedding and the making of our beds.

In the next letter to my family which began on Monday, April 14th, I made this statement:

> I haven't much to say about this camp and army life, except as yet I don't like it! Today is Wednesday. I didn't have time to write Tuesday because we were in K.P. (Kitchen Police) duty for fourteen hours. Getting up at four, getting ready by five a.m. and then working until seven p.m., I was really tired.

I remained at Fort McDowell for the next five days where I wrote lots of letters which "helped ease the awful homesickness that made me feel as if I wanted to cry. We leave for Corregidor on Monday, April 21." [2] (A post card written on the 22nd stated that the ship was leaving later in the afternoon.)

When I boarded the luxury ocean liner the USS *Washington*, which had been converted into a troop transport, I was told

---

1. McGarry, Wendell H., talk at Manti High School, Manti Utah, Veteran's Day, 1993.
2. McGarry, Wendell H., letter, Fort McDowell, CA, April 19, 1941.

that she and her sister ship the *Manhattan* were the largest commercial ships in the U.S.A. There were several hundred military personnel aboard who were also being shipped into the South Pacific. The luxurious ocean-going ship was still very beautiful, but it was now packed with hundreds of young American men who had just put their civilian lives on hold, and who were gearing up for war.

Along with dozens of other guys I would not enjoy my first cruise to Hawaii. The accommodations left a lot to be desired. My bunk was the sixth one up in the empty swimming pool. The company was rowdy and the food I ate was awful because I was seasick, violently ill at first. There was not really anything to do except read, write letters or gamble which I did not want to do, so I volunteered to help swab the decks just to break up the routine. I swore that I would never board another ship except the one that would take me back to the good old U.S.A.!

Early in the morning on Saturday, April 26th, after four days of sailing from San Francisco, we docked at the pier in beautiful Pearl Harbor in the Hawaiian Islands. I remember being totally amazed at the reception we received.

Before we came into the harbor there were several Army planes that dove, circled and dove again over the Washington. The water became a flurry of activity with numerous small motor boats filled with passengers in a very festive mode who waved and shouted their welcome as they circled the ship. Bands played and the shore was lined with pretty Hawaiian girls whose arms were loaded with "necklaces" of flowers which were put around passenger's necks as they walked onto shore. Young boys were swimming around the ship, shouting for those aboard to throw coins into the water, then diving to retrieve them.[3]

We were allowed to go ashore. A letter written from Hawaii to my family said:

> We spent two wonderful days on Waikiki, the most beautiful beach, and swimming in the bluest water I have ever seen.

This was where a good share of the servicemen disembarked. They would be stationed at different military bases—Hickham

---

3. McGarry, Wendell H., letter, Hawaii, April 6, 1941.

Field and Pearl Harbor Naval Base, to mention a couple. "What a tour of duty that would be!" I thought.

The rest of us aboard ship were bound for the Philippines where different contingents were to serve at bases on Luzon Island including Fort McKinley, Clark Field, Nicholes Field, and the Cavite Naval Base as well as those of us who were to be stationed on Corregidor at Fort Mills. Only then did I have my own stateroom—a very nice change in accommodations for the remainder of the trip. It would take several more days of sailing to reach the Philippines.

After my arrival I learned that Corregidor Island was the largest of the four fortified islands in Manila Bay. Measuring just one-half mile across at the widest point, it contains a mere three and one-half square miles. The Island is shaped like a tadpole the length of which runs four miles east and west with the South China Sea to the west. Manila the Philippine capital city, lies to the north-east twenty-six miles. The Cavite Naval Base is ten miles away across the south channel and the Bataan Peninsula lies five miles north across the north channel.

Three smaller islands where American bases were located were Caballo, or Fort Hughes; El Fraile, or Fort Drum; and Carabao or Fort Frank. All of them volcanic rock formations whose fortifications were designed to guard the entrance to Manila Bay.[4]

It was a lush green the first time I saw the "Rock" rising majestically out of the tepid Manila Bay waters on May 8, 1941. Tropical in climate and beautiful, especially so in the eyes of a twenty-three year old soldier who had been raised in the dry desert state of Utah. The days would prove to be hot and humid but when the heat of day melted away and the evenings cooled somewhat with the ocean breezes I was reminded of the beautiful summer nights at home in Utah.

The ship had docked at the Army wharves on the north side of the island where we were billeted in tents. We were promptly quarantined for a couple of weeks to insure that we had all received the proper immunizations as well as to be certain we

---

4. Corregidor. Alfonzo J. Aluit, *Galleon Guide Book*, 1980, Zone Printing Co. Inc. Caloocan City, P.I. 8.

were not playing host to any communicable diseases. Subsequent letters to my family told of my daily activities:

> We spend our time drilling, eating out of canteen equipment with food thrown in, in Mulligan stew fashion, and sleeping in this section of the island away from all other soldiers on the island.

> I just have six more days before I go to the hospital for regular duty and I really can't wait, because everything I've done so far has made me feel very blue and homesick. But I know you're thinking of me, so it makes me feel quite a bit better. If it wasn't that I missed everyone at home so very much—I think I'd like it here—but no matter how much I like it, I'll never stay any longer than I have to because it just isn't what I want.

> I just celebrated my first month in the Army May 10 by marching myself stiff and then I spent most of the night looking at a beautiful big moon, thinking of home and all my brothers and sisters. I was sort of satisfied to think that the same moon would soon shine again on them.[5]

> On May 21 we were allowed to go to "Topside" which is located on a plateau formed on the head of the tadpole shaped rock. It is the area where the Fort Mills headquarters as well as the hospital where I will be working are located. I was somewhat surprised to see a theatre, but very excited to see the beautiful, very well maintained nine-hole golf course. I wish I had my clubs. There are officer's quarters in addition to enlisted men's barracks which are very large. There are many gun emplacements on Topside with huge guns. I have not seen them, but have been told that there are underground facilities of some sort as well.[6]

A light rail system, to which we had easy access we found to be quite reliable, connected the different areas of Corregidor Island. It was widely used by the military personnel as well as the civilian Filipino population who lived in the two barrios, (villages) San Jose and San Isidoro.

5. McGarry, Wendell H., letter from Corregidor, May 10, 1941.
6. McGarry, Wendell H., letter from Corregidor, May 21, 1942.

Most of the men settled into the four-story concrete-and-steel reinforced barracks which were referred to as the longest barracks in the world and were purported to be bomb-proof, a statement that was proven to be a fallacy during the Japanese bombings. (Concrete skeletons of these structures, nearly overgrown with tropical vegetation and dissected by vine-encircled trees growing through the dilapidated floors and roof were all that remained of these once imposing barracks in 1982.)[7]

Those of us who were medical personnel were located in quarters close to the hospital. I found a bunk near a window and stowed my gear. As I looked outside I saw beautifully manicured, vibrant green lawns, shrubs and trees surrounding clean, neatly maintained buildings. And there was this delicious fragrance, one that I couldn't quite identify, wafting on the tropical breeze coming through the open window.

This was a moment to be remembered, to be filed away in the recesses of my psyche, to help ease the nostalgia I felt for my home and my family, and to be recalled countless times over the next three hellish years.

On investigation I found that the heady odor I was experiencing was coming from a tree-sized gardenia bush located just outside the window close to the barracks' wall. The bush was covered with delicate, creamy-white blossoms. The soft, velvet-like petals formed gorgeous three-inch flowers with a fragrance to die for.

I closed my eyes and remembered feeling the delightful sensation of gliding around the dance floor of the South High School gymnasium in Salt Lake City. I was at the senior prom with an armful of a special little blond named Mary Louise Miller and she was wearing a fragrant gardenia corsage.

This sweet, simple pleasure was mine. Mornings I awakened to begin the day with the unmistakable gardenia fragrance in my nostrils, evenings after taps a warm tropical breeze laced with the heavenly gardenia perfume lulled me into a safe, secure sleep.

The experience with the gardenia, its fragrance and the feelings that were mine then, would provide mental and

---

7. McGarry observation of the barracks as we visited Corregidor in 1998.

emotional sustenance to me at difficult periods of time when there were none. My physical pain would become less severe and my spiritual and emotional despair would ease somewhat with this pleasant memory.

More than sixty years later, I continue to enjoy those pleasant sensations with the sight and smell of the eternally beautiful flower—my favorite—the gardenia.

– 2 –

NINE MONTHS OF PEACE

After my induction into the ranks of the "Old Army," the realization came quite rapidly that my life and the way I had been living it was in the process of a drastic change. I was one who had come and gone at will, indulging in occasional weekend recreational activities and wearing what I chose, be it casual or more of a Sunday-go-to-meeting attire. Until it was gone, I failed to realize that I had taken my independence for granted.

Although difficult, I studied hard and worked many hours to graduate from high school and through more than three years at the University of Utah. I rode the bus to the U for 7:00 am to 11:00 am classes every morning and worked a twelve-hour day from noon to midnight in the produce department at a local market. After arriving home, I studied until the wee hours of the morning to prepare my assignments and would eventually fall exhausted into bed. It was not easy but it had been my choice.

I now belonged to an organization of strong, tough, sometimes mean-spirited men who indulged in rudeness and crude jargon with expectations of superhuman conduct, especially from new recruits. We were yelled at, belittled and often pushed beyond the limits of our human endurance. We learned very rapidly to observe immediate, strict obedience to the rules of protocol, never questioning the wisdom or the logic of an order. We did as we were told. That was basic training. After this short but miserable time was completed, conditions became much more pleasant.

However, as the weeks literally melted into the hot, humid months of summer, I found myself feeling extremely lonely and homesick. I hated the rainy season when it was upon us. It rained all the time. Nights I crawled into a bed that felt like the sheets were still wet from the laundry when the bed was made up. Days were gloomy, overcast and so steamy hot. Even the ocean breezes weren't able to dispel the dank, stifling humidity. Give me dry old Utah any day.

I didn't like the army, the strict discipline, the regimentation and I hated being in a foreign country so far from my family. Having been raised the fourth son and the sixth child in a family of nine siblings, I was used to being part of a close-knit union. We worked together, played together, and we completely enjoyed the relationships of parents, brothers and sisters who understood and loved each other. I had almost forgotten the degree of loneliness I felt at that time until after the war when I read the letters I had sent home to my parents.

Mother had saved all of them and in almost every one I literally counted the months, weeks, and days left on Corregidor to fulfill my two-year hitch in the army. I suppose it was a good thing I had no idea I would be spending three more years in the Philippine Islands as a prisoner of the Japanese.

I was very fortunate to have received pre-med training before the war, as it was the deciding factor in my assignment to work in the medical supply room at the hospital. I was learning so much about medications as well as becoming acquainted with the instruments used in the medical profession. I planned to continue my education in dentistry when my commitment to the military was completed. Later in the summer I moved into the dental clinic where I trained as a dental technician. There I worked closely with the dentists learning hands-on techniques. The work was enjoyable and I was most grateful for this special opportunity. Then, too, my schedule was from 7:30 am to 3:00 pm five days a week with a half-day on Saturday. Sunday I had off. It couldn't have been any better than that.

As I adjusted to the routine on Corregidor, I began to appreciate the fact that there was an upside to all the downside I didn't like about my situation. I didn't need to worry about any logistics. When my eight-hour shift was finished, I ate dinner in the hospital where food was prepared by army mess cooks. The fare hardly compared to the good cooking of my mother, but it wasn't too bad after a day's work and I didn't have to prepare it. (Medical personnel never pulled KP duty.)

The remainder of the evening was spent indulging in a poker game if I were lucky enough to have any money to wager. Or I could read. I very much enjoyed reading good books or a magazine. On one occasion I remember being completely excited while reading a detective magazine. The article was about a murder being solved by a detective from the Salt Lake City Police Department. He was the dad of a good friend of mine and he worked with my dad who was a member of that same police force. The article almost made me feel closer to home.

Occasionally, some of the guys and I enjoyed a good movie at the base theatre, mostly entertaining musicals full of beautiful girls that left all of us feeling good but a bit nostalgic for home and female companionship.

There were no dates, as the only women available were nurses who were commissioned officers and protocol was strictly enforced forbidding officers fraternizing with enlisted men.

I coveted the golf course which was also off limits to enlisted men. Only officers were allowed to play. I had been raised across the street from a golf course in Salt Lake City and began to caddy when I was eleven or twelve. By the time I was grown I had become hopelessly entangled in a lifelong love affair with golf. I hated not being able to tee off, drive the fairways, and putt those beautiful greens.

Early in the morning we were awakened by the bugle's reveille call, followed by the chirping of countless tropical birds. And there was the delicious odor of the gardenia bush outside my window, which helped stem the tide of irritation created by the noisy bugle.

After a quick shower, I walked to the hospital and ate breakfast, my bed left unmade and soiled laundry dropped on the floor. The housekeeping chores were attended to by Filipino men who slept in our barracks and who were happy to do the household chores for a pittance. The laundry was taken to the barrio or village where Filipino women washed, starched, and pressed the uniforms to army protocol perfection. The socks and underwear were neatly folded and returned to our barracks ready to wear. This was also done for a small amount of pay. But then, our wages were comparably small. However, it was great not to have to do these menial tasks myself.

Payday came once a month. In retrospect it all seems kind of comical. There was this long table where the paymaster sat and divvied out the pay as the soldier's name was called. We were paid in Filipino pesos where we received two pesos for one American dollar. For the first three months, a buck private earned $21.00 per month or forty-two pesos. Then his pay went up to $30.00 per month. A corporal earned a whopping $54.00. Of course the pay scale went up from there according to rank.

The good news came when payday rolled around. The bad news came along with it when all the fees were deducted. Insurance costs came out, then there was the laundry and housekeeping expense. If a person smoked, $2.00 a carton for cigarettes was taken out, which usually amounted to $6.00 for a pack a day for a month. If we ran out of money before the end of the month, and most of us did, whatever amount had been borrowed had to be repaid. If there was anything left it amounted to "chicken feed." I didn't mind too much if I had little or no money left. My needs and wants were on the meager side.

Weekends when I was not on duty at the hospital a couple of buddies and I would board the train and traverse the island. We were not restricted as to where we could go except the off-limits gun battery emplacements and a G2 intelligence radio facility at Monkey Point, which was located at the extreme end of the island.

Occasionally we would go to the San Jose barrio where we made purchases. Eventually all of us would buy a suit which was made to order from sharkskin. Expertly hand tailored, they were light and comfortably cool to wear in the tropical heat. Also, civilian shoes were available made to order and very reasonable in price.

Having been raised as a member of the Church of Jesus Christ of Latter-day Saints, or the Mormon Church as it is commonly called, I would have attended church on Sunday, but there were no LDS services held on the island. I attended a service held by the Protestant Church a couple of times. Most often the day was spent in the barracks beside the open window enjoying the fragrant gardenia-scented breeze and listening to a radio airing a San Francisco station. I enjoyed hearing the Big Band music while I read, wrote letters home, or just relaxed.

When I arrived on Corregidor I had forty American dollars in my pocket. Having been quite frugal the first few months, I had managed to save enough additional money to allow for a three-day pass to Manila to do some sight-seeing. I was anxious to visit Intramuros, the Walled City which was built by the Spanish, the famous Manila Hotel, and the Royal Malacanang Palace. Then, too, there were beautiful silks and hand-made gifts to send home to my family.

A new recruit was not allowed to make this first trip into the capital city alone. He was to be accompanied by a non-commissioned officer who was given the ultimatum to accomplish three things or he would lose his stripes. First, he was to get his charge drunk; second, show him a good time; and third, bring him back safely.

The first of my many trips to Manila before the war came in July 1941. Corporal Cruson was my escort. He was killed in 1944 on Palawan Island when the Japanese herded one hundred and fifty POWs into underground air raid shelters that had been doused with gasoline, then set on fire. As the prisoners ran out they were cut down by machine guns. Only a handful of men escaped this carnage.

The first trip I made to Manila after the war began was on June 30, 1943. I was a Prisoner of War. I was paraded through streets lined with cheering Filipinos, along with dozens of my fellow POWs and we were escorted by our Japanese captors.

THE WAR BEGINS

It was almost noon, 11:54 am, December 29, 1941. The comparative peace and calm of Fort Mills on Corregidor Island was shattered by the crescendo and incessant screaming of air-raid sirens.

I had been at work since early morning in the Fort Mills hospital along with the other medical personnel. We heard the drone of enemy bombers and suddenly the sky was filled with planes and bombs exploded all around us. The war had finally come to Corregidor. Dust, acrid smoke, and flying debris filled the air. Flames belched forth from wooden structures, quickly reducing them to charred ashes. The thunderous noise threatened our eardrums and the tendrils of concussion tightened around our innards. All hell was breaking loose! The underside of the winged aircraft carried the rising sun emblem of the Imperial Japanese Air Force.

I was more scared than I had ever been in my whole life. My heart was beating very loud, I wondered if everyone could hear it. My mouth was so dry, I couldn't even spit. I knew immediately my God. The Lord is my Shepherd, and I remember the prayers that my Mother had taught me as I knelt by my bed; if I should die before I wake. I prayed desperately, please, God, don't let the ones I love at home suffer or worry too much over me. Help me to do what I need to do. Please, help me to not let down in command or performance.[8]

---

8. McGarry talk, Manti High School.

On December 8th (December 7th in Hawaii) we had been awakened early by a sergeant who burst excitedly into the barracks. Shouting as he raced between the bunks, laying a quirt (riding whip) sharply across the backsides of the sleeping soldiers, "Hit the deck! The dirty, rotten Japs have just attacked Pearl Harbor!"

Thousands of miles away in the Hawaiian Islands, the American Naval Base, Pearl Harbor, had been bombed, destroying a significant share of fighting vessels in the United States Navy. Nine American battleships were sunk or damaged when nineteen of the enemy aerial torpedoes struck their targets. Among them were the *West Virginia*, sunk at her berth, the *Tennessee*, badly damaged, and the *Arizona*, sunk at her berth, carrying with her 1,102 entombed crew members to her watery grave.

The *Nevada*, hit by a single torpedo, was further damaged when struck by five bombs as she attempted to clear the Harbor. To prevent blocking the channel, she was beached. The *Oklahoma* capsized and sank within twenty minutes of being hit by four torpedoes. The battleship *California* sank at her berth three days after being badly damaged. The lucky battleship USS *Maryland* sustained only slight damage.

The deck of the ex-battleship the USS *Utah* had been stripped and she was being used as a training target ship. From the air she resembled the flight deck of a carrier and was sunk when struck by three torpedoes. The bodies of fifty-eight Navy men who lost their lives aboard the *Utah* remain in the destroyed hulk.

The USS *Pennsylvania*, the Pacific Fleet's flag ship, moored in dry dock at the Naval Shipyard, was bombed and damaged along with two destroyers. All of the eighteen vessels which were sunk at Pearl Harbor that fateful Sunday morning were later re-floated except the *Arizona* and the *Utah*.

The attack on Pearl Harbor resulted in the loss of 3,067 American servicemen. Many of them were also killed in the bombing of Hickham Field the Army's Air base, the Marine

Corps Air Station, Kanoehe Naval Air Station and several others. Most of the aircraft were destroyed as well.[9]

The peace of the beautiful, tropical Sunday morning suddenly and without warning metamorphosed into the raging inferno of hell. Shortly the resounding cry, "Remember Pearl Harbor" would reverberate with anger and indignation around the world![10]

Luzon Island across Manila Bay had undergone a similar attack the same day. Camp John Hay in Baguio City, located on Northern Luzon, had been bombarded by Japanese aircraft. Davao City on the southern Island of Mindanao had come under fire. Other islands in the Philippine archipelago were also attacked. Just after noon, Clark Field, located in Angeles, Pampanga on Luzon Island, which was known as the major US Air Base in the Far East, was bombed and strafed. Like the ships in Pearl Harbor that were disabled and sunk at their docks, most of the planes at Clark Field were totally destroyed where they rested on the ground.[11]

The attack had been anticipated, but the devastation and carnage which resulted from the bombing bore stark evidence that complete preparation for such an event had not been in place.

During the nine months I was stationed at Fort Mills, there had been significant preparations made to put the island in readiness for an attack. Some new installations had been built, and training of both American and Filipino troops was done. However, we were totally lacking in good equipment and munitions. Most of it dated back to WW I.

For days now we had been able to see the fires and the resultant destruction of the exploding bombs on the Bataan Peninsula from across the bay. The war we had witnessed from

---

9. "Adventure 5." Brochure for Pearl Harbor Cruise. Graphic description of Japanese attack on Pearl Harbor December 7, 1941.
10. Corregidor. The Fall, Sol L. Villa, *Chronicle Magazine*, Vol. XXII, N0. 18. Manila, Philippines, 7. This publication contained a graphic and detailed account of the events leading to the Fall of Corregidor and was purchased in May, 1967 when Wendell returned to the Philippines with his wife Donna for the 25th Anniversary Commemoration of the Fall. Hereafter referred to as the *Chronicle Magazine*.
11. Gene Jacobson personal interview, St. George, Utah, January 2003. Jacobsen was stationed at Clark A.F.B. and later became a survivor of the Bataan Death March.

a comparatively safe distance was now upon us. On Monday, December 29th, the expectations of war became reality and hit us right between the eyes.

The island was disintegrating; structures of all kinds burst into flame. The twin-engine bombers dropped tons of bombs for a full thirty minutes. About 12:30 a second wave of light bombers came in and dropped their loads of devastation on Topside and Middleside. They were almost immediately followed by a group of dive bombers, followed closely by a squadron of some sixty Japanese navy bombers, dropping their loads of destruction, strafing the targets, then finally flying away.

This was considered the heaviest aerial attack Corregidor Island was subjected to during WW II. It lasted just two hours. However, the episode had been very costly to the Japanese as they had lost thirteen medium bombers and four dive bombers.[12] The island anti-aircraft guns had done their work quite effectively in spite of the heavy air bombardment.

After the first attack had stopped for a few minutes, I was sent out with a driver on an ambulance to pick up any wounded and transport them to the hospital in the Malinta Tunnel located in the Malinta Hills.

Southeast of Bottomside on the Island of Corregidor, the Malinta Hills form the body of the tadpole-shaped island. Construction of the tunnels began in 1922 and they were designed as storage rooms for the strategic materials stockpiled on the island. The principal tunnel, which is considered to be an engineering marvel, is more than nine hundred twenty-five feet long, twenty-five feet wide, and eighteen feet high at the top of the arched roof. It was virtually completed in 1922. Extending from the sides of this tunnel were twenty-four main laterals, thirteen on the north side and eleven on the south. Each lateral averaged one hundred-sixty feet long and fifteen feet wide."[13]

The second lateral to the north side from the east entrance led into another group of twelve laterals which served as the Fort Mills Hospital during the siege of Corregidor. Ten of the

---

12. *Chronicle Magazine*, 7.
13. Ibid.

laterals had a capacity of one hundred beds each. One of the other two laterals housed the nurses. The enlisted men who worked in the hospital were housed in the other one. The third lateral on the north side from the east entrance also served as the United Stated Armed Forces in the Far East Headquarters (USAFFE) of General Douglas MacArthur. The general, his wife, and son Arthur were briefly housed here along with his staff until March 11, 1942 when they all left for Australia upon orders from President Franklin D. Roosevelt. General Jonathan Wainwright then took command of all US forces in the Philippines.[14]

The President of the Philippines, Manuel L. Quezon, his wife, two daughters, and some of his staff had also been housed in the Malinta Tunnel from December 1941 to February 1942 when they were transferred to the United States.[15]

Shortly after leaving the Fort Mills Hospital, we found ourselves in the middle of the second attack. We were stopped by military police and directed to the first battery we found. I don't remember which one we took cover in until the air raids were over. While we huddled in the comparative safety of the battery with bombs crashing about us, hell bent on the complete destruction of the island fortress, for the first time in my life I considered the possibility I might be going to die. Soon. In fact, during or before this air raid was over, the probability that it could happen was in the ninety-nine percentile.

I remembered the times that my dad had tried to give me advice and I wished that I had paid more attention to what he said. I wished I hadn't said "Oh Mom," every time she hugged me and tried to make sure my hair was combed and I was dressed properly before leaving for school. And how I wished I hadn't fought so often with my brothers and sisters. Then I remembered the kiss of the girl I had left behind, the sweet, salty taste of her tears as she begged me to return.

I got a lot smarter real fast when I realized my life depended on others and they depended on me for theirs. Then I thought

---

14. Ibid., 6.
15. Ibid., 7

of all the opportunities that I had let slide by while I was at home and still in school. All of these things raced through my mind before that first day of battle was over while the bombs were still falling and hell was raging all around me.[16]

We were never able to deliver any wounded to the Malinta Tunnel hospital after the attack ceased as the ambulance had disappeared. We finally made our way to the hospital to await further orders where I would work for the next five months until the fall of Corregidor.

The destruction on the island continued to accelerate. The so-called "bomb proof" barracks which were built of concrete several feet thick were damaged extensively. The post headquarters, the evacuated hospital building, the officer's club, and two water tank systems were nearly destroyed.[17]

And there were casualties, lots of casualties. The Malinta Tunnel hospital was filling up fast. The surgical and nursing staffs were worked to exhaustion. My duties at the hospital varied. I was assigned to work in the dental clinic as well as in the operating room. I was also on call to go into the field to retrieve casualties whenever there was a need.

One day while I was on duty, a wounded 2nd lieutenant was brought in accompanied by a colonel whom I immediately recognized. Colonel Brighton had been CO of the ROTC unit I belonged to while attending my first two years of college at Utah State University in Logan, Utah.

I approached the colonel and told him who I was and what our relationship had been at USU. He seemed happy to see someone from "home," so to speak. We chatted briefly, then he astounded me with a request. He told me he wanted me to take the place of the wounded 2nd lieutenant he had brought into the hospital. He was the colonel's personal aid, and he wanted me—now. He would see to it that I received a 2nd Lieutenant field commission.

Upon hearing what sounded almost like an order, the doctor who was in charge of the hospital gave him a very firm, "No, we have too many critically wounded patients here needing immediate care and I can't spare the corporal."

16. McGarry talk, Manti High School.
17. *Chronicle Magazine*, 7.

I thanked Colonel Brighton, telling him I appreciated the opportunity, but I was committed to stay where I was so badly needed. He turned on his heel and left without another word.

When I first arrived on Corregidor in the spring of 1941, I had heard that Colonel Brighton was stationed on Topside. I received permission to go to his headquarters for a visit. I spoke to a lieutenant colonel who was his second in command. For some reason, he refused to let me see Colonel Brighton. I left, disappointed and a little angry at the rejection. As I turned to leave the lieutenant colonel reminded me that I had forgotten to salute him. I apologized, saluted, and went on my way. I didn't expect to see Colonel Brighton after that incident, especially under these most interesting circumstances.

Perhaps my guardian angel was on duty that day protecting me from the fate that Colonel Brighton and his aid suffered at Cabanatuan sometime later. I was told that he, along with several other officers, had attempted to escape. When they were apprehended, Colonel Brighton was shot and his 2nd lieutenant aid was beheaded by the Japanese.

Despite the barrage of artillery fire from the well camouflaged gun emplacements on Cavite and Bataan, Corregidor was enduring. The largest guns on Topside, Battery Geary, and Battery Crockett had received minimal damage and were still presenting a formidable defense against the enemy. Their deadly accuracy against these particular emplacements was substantially increased after the reconnaissance flight of a lone unarmed P26 aircraft. Captain Jesus Villamor, a Filipino war ace, received his second Distinguished Service Cross for the photographs of enemy emplacements he took on that extremely precarious historic flight.[18]

On the 5th of February, 1942, the artillery bombardment of Corregidor began in earnest. Coupled with the air attacks, the assault took its toll and the defenses of Corregidor were losing strength. By the first week in March the final drive to defeat Bataan was launched by the Japanese. At about that time, Corregidor received more attention from the enemy as well.[19]

18. Ibid.
19. Ibid.

I remember an incident which took place sometime in mid-April during one of my details into the battle field to pick up wounded. We were on the hills above the outside hospital entrance into the Malinta Tunnel. I had a squad of men with me, eight litter bearers and two litters. We were preparing to pick up the wounded when I heard the distinctive whine of a mortar shell headed our way.

As we all dove for cover, out of the corner of my eye I saw this officer standing straight up looking around as if nothing was happening. I swore under my breath, jumped up, and hit the idiot in the back, knocking him to the ground as I shouted, "Get down, you stupid son-of-a-bitch!" The shell exploded far enough away that no one was hurt, but we were showered with debris.

Opening my eyes, I recoiled in horror when I saw the shiny Silver Star on the shoulder tab directly beneath my chin. "Holy hell!" I thought, "I've knocked the general on his ass I'll be court-martialed for sure!"

As I helped General George Moore, my commanding officer, to his feet while extending my most humble apology, I was petrified. Ignoring my confused attempts to say how sorry I was, he quietly asked for my name, rank and serial number. Then he thanked me. I was completely stunned when he said, "I've always been more afraid of public opinion than I am of being killed by the enemy."

In the ensuing weeks during the siege of Corregidor, I had many opportunities to meet and gradually get to know General Moore. He always greeted me with warmth when he came into the dental clinic where I was working, "Good morning Corporal McGarry," or "How are things with you today?" My interaction with the General became one of mutual respect bordering on friendship, a relationship I would cherish in the difficult days ahead and would thank my guardian angel for fostering.

The war raged in all its fury around us for nearly four months. The scream of falling high altitude bombs and the whining of approaching mortar shells from across the bay were nerve-racking to say the least. But most of the time we were too busy to notice. The flow of wounded into the Malinta Tunnel hospital was continuous and unrelenting. We were all extremely tired, but luckily, supplies and medications were still in fairly good supply.

The latter part of April I was working in the operating room. The main hospital tunnel just outside of the lateral containing the dental clinic and the operating room (OR) was where the wounded were deposited when they were brought in from the field. When patients were brought in for surgery, they were placed on the floor still on the litter. Nurses removed their clothing and placed it in a bundle on the floor. It was my job to remove all of the effects from the clothes, inventory them, place everything into large manila envelopes, then file the envelopes in alphabetical order according to the man's name in a drawer in one of three filing cabinets.

The most prized possession a soldier had at this time were cigarettes. I was very careful to make sure they were all accounted for and they were safe from pilfering. The money I found was of no value. There was no one to spend it on and nowhere to go to have a good time.

One day, a 2nd Lieutenant Bliss came in as a patient. I was told he was the son of Colonel Bliss. I treated his effects in the same manner I did everyone else and stored them in the filing cabinet. However, he had in his possession a pouch which contained a lot of Filipino pesos. I learned later it was the company payroll. I also found out it was strictly against protocol for an enlisted man to handle payroll funds.

Shortly after I had taken care of Lieutenant Bliss's effects, a sergeant came into the surgery and told me that I was to take a squad, eight men and two litters, up the hill to the searchlight facility behind the hospital tunnel entrance. There were wounded there who needed to be brought in for treatment. As we neared the searchlight location, I could see smoke and flames belching out of the tunnel where the searchlight crew would have been working. I was sick at the sight, knowing full well that there was no possibility anyone could have survived a fire of that intensity from the direct hit on the installation.

A colonel, the officer in charge, was extremely agitated and he shouted, "Get the hell in there and get those men out."

I said, "No, sir, I won't send my men in there. Those guys are already dead and I won't risk the lives of anyone else."

The colonel was livid. "You dare to disobey a direct order?" he bellowed.

"Yes, sir," I replied.

"Name, rank and serial number!" he barked, scarlet faced, neck veins bulging. He interrupted my reply with, "I'll kill you, you son-of-a-bitch!" With that he jerked his handgun from his side holster, and aimed it right between my eyes.

Immediately, another officer standing nearby grabbed hold of the colonel and turned his back to me. At the same instant, a third officer stepped up, put his face in mine and ordered, "Get your ass out of here now!" I didn't need to be told twice.

When I arrived back at the hospital, word of the incident at the searchlight was already circulating. I was greeted by several of the "Old Army" guys who were deeply concerned. "Good hell, Mac! You refused to obey a direct order? What in the devil were you thinking?" asked one.

"You're in deep trouble this time!" volunteered another.

Of course, I knew that the punishment for refusing to obey a direct order in wartime was execution, but I believed I had done the only thing I could do to protect my men under the circumstances. "To hell with a court-martial," I thought rebelliously.

A while later I looked up from what I was doing. General Moore came through the dental clinic and walked over to me, a grave look on his face. "We need to talk."

I immediately blurted out my account of the searchlight fiasco and finished with, "What the hell am I going to do? Will I be court-martialed?"

He almost smiled as he said, "Don't worry about that, Corporal. I'll take care of it. But that isn't what I came here to talk to you about." I was totally confused! Then the General continued, "Remember Lieutenant Bliss who came into the OR this morning?"

"Yes sir," I replied.

"Was it you who took care of his personal effects before he went into surgery?" I answered in the affirmative. Then the General asked, "Didn't you know it's against protocol for an enlisted man to handle the company payroll?"

Totally amazed, I replied, "No sir, I didn't know. I inventoried his belongings just like I do everyone else who comes into the OR. I had no idea all the money was the payroll. I was just doing my job."

"Show me where you put the money, Corporal."

I took the general to the area where the filing cabinets stood, opened a drawer, and pulled out the manila envelope with Lieutenant Bliss' name on it. The pouch full of money that was with it was gone! I was aghast! "That's where it was when I left to go to the searchlight," I groaned, sick at heart.

General Moore calmed me down when he told me he already knew where the payroll was. Colonel Cooper, the officer in charge of the hospital, had been informed that Lieutenant Bliss was carrying it when he was brought into the OR. The colonel had come into the hospital and retrieved the money, then he reported to the general how it got there and who was responsible for it.

I was beside myself with worry. One count of ignoring the protocol was bad enough, but two infractions would sure as hell get me the death penalty.

General Moore put his hand on my shoulder, looked into my eyes, and said, "There will be a court-martial hearing probably tomorrow." Almost smiling, he said, "I know you, Corporal, and I've found you to be quite reliable and responsible. In my opinion you acted appropriately in both instances. I don't think you had a choice." Then General Moore dropped a bombshell on me. He said quite nonchalantly, "Don't worry about the court-martial, Corporal. Do you know who makes the final decision in these trials? The commanding officer does and you know who that is?" Jerking his thumb at his chest, "Me!"

Even though I was a bit apprehensive, I was totally relieved. I felt my guardian angel had indeed been working overtime.

Both incidents were completely ignored and soon forgotten, except for the "Old Army" buddies of mine who were at a loss to explain how in the hell I had escaped being shot at sunrise. I sort of answered their puzzled inquiries when I smiled and said, "Just lucky, I guess.

4

THE FALL OF CORREGIDOR—MAY 6, 1942

The capitulation of Bataan occurred at 6:00 am Thursday, April 9, 1942. General Edward King Jr., who was the commander of the Fil-American forces on Bataan, ordered all units to destroy equipment and supplies, after which they were to surrender. He then sued for truce. For those Americans on Bataan who had fought so long and gallantly, the war was over, but the nightmare of the Japanese occupation had just begun.

Almost immediately the air raids and the ground assault of mortar fire on Corregidor resumed at a much more intense and accelerated pace. It was under constant attack almost around the clock. The Japanese were throwing all that they had, including ground troops, at the Rock fortress to bring about the unconditional surrender of Corregidor. When this occurred, the victory for the invading Japanese army in the Philippine Islands would be complete. They had anticipated this would happen very quickly and without much of a fight.

For twenty-seven long, bloody days, men of the United States Armed Forces stubbornly fought and died. Knowing there was no hope of any outside help, they courageously faced the challenges the enemy threw at them. They fought valiantly with all of the ebbing strength of a wounded she-lion. Their tenacity defied and outraged the adversary.[20]

The Malinta Tunnel hospital was full to overflowing. We worked to the point of total exhaustion, then we worked some

20. *Chronicle Magazine*, 10.

more. All the main tunnel laterals were choked with refugees who had escaped from Bataan as well as those streaming in from Topside, Middleside, and Bottomside. Wounded who were brought in by medics, friends, and anyone else who happened to find them, filled the main tunnel outside of the hospital lateral. Food and water were becoming a premium.

When there was a slight lull in the bombing and shelling, I would take a squad of men with two litters and go outside the tunnel to retrieve the wounded. There were always more patients than we could pick up in a matter of a few minutes. We tried to bring in the ones whose wounds appeared such that the patient would survive if given immediate treatment. The others would have to wait until we made the next trip outside or until someone else came to their rescue.

Each bone-weary day was filled with blood, cries of agonizing pain, and death. The thousand beds in the hospital were filled and patients were sitting or lying all around on the floor. Many of them were just waiting, for what they had no idea, and furthermore, they didn't really care.

I suppose I hadn't realized what the long hours, insufficient rest and stress I had been under was doing to me physically. One morning I awoke from a short, troubled sleep feeling lightheaded, aching in every bone in my body. After struggling to shower and grab a cup of coffee, I hurried to get back into the hospital where they were desperately short of help.

One of the nurses almost ran into me as I entered the hospital lateral. When she looked at me she exclaimed, "McGarry, what's the matter with you? You look like hell!" I tried to convince her I was all right, but in the process I almost passed out. Immediately, she escorted me to an empty bed, and demanded I undress and get into it. I had a nasty case of dengue fever which plagued me for several days with an elevated temperature and extremely uncomfortable bone-crushing pain throughout my entire body.

The side effects were good, however, as I was the object of tender loving care on the part of all the nurses on duty. Not because they loved me, but because they needed my help and they did everything in their power to encourage a speedy recovery. Although still a bit shaky I was back to work a couple of days later.

Rumors of a ground invasion by the enemy were circulating through the Malinta Tunnel, but we had received no official word it was about to happen. Then the Japanese air attacks from the 29th of April to May 1st doubled in intensity. "Immediately the Japanese heavy artillery installations from Mt. Sumat and Caviti began to rain shells on the fortress with unrelenting, deadly fury."[21] The horrific noise and the concussion from the blasts made it even more difficult for us to continue care of the many patients.

On the 2nd of May, a direct hit on the ammunition magazine of Battery Geary rocked the whole island with a thunderous explosion that threatened to split the Rock asunder. This dealt the final, crippling blow to the defense of the island fortress.[22]

Despite the feelings of impending doom, and the shadow of defeat looming near, the steadfast Americans troops continued their courageous struggle to stand their ground. Even as the too-numerous Japanese invaders literally mowed them down, pulverizing and destroying everything in their path of vicious destruction, shoving them rapidly into imminent annihilation, still with desperate determination not to give up, they continued to fight!

The tropical world in which I lived for more than a year had become dear to my heart and was rapidly being destroyed. I could do nothing but wait and try not to think about it.

At the culmination of another very long, difficult day I retired to my quarters for a few hours and penned the following letters to my mother. On Thursday April 30, 1942 I wrote:

> Dearest Mother,
>
> As you can imagine by my letters, you have constantly been in—or rather on my mind. It probably isn't the best thing to do, because it makes you so discontented. But no matter what you do, you can't stop it. Simply because there are so many things here that cry out to you the great difference.
>
> The once green and beautiful land is now turned greenish brown. The trees are being ripped and blown down. So

---

21. *Chronicle Magazine*, 10.
22. Ibid.

instead of a beautiful South Sea heaven where once birds twittered and the sea splashed and laughed, as it rolled back and forth, you have nothing beautiful here now, nothing unless one could call being able to watch these events and live through it—beautiful.

So you see, Mother dearest, it's these, plus many other things, that make you very, very homesick and nearer to your "God." I'm writing this rather hurriedly because it is going out tonight.

Say hello to them all for me, Mom, all my brothers and sisters.

My life around here now, strange as it may seem, isn't very rigid, nor very hard. For it still is in the same line as it always has been. The only things however, that don't agree with me are these dishes of rice. Boy, rice for every meal! It's really tough, but not so much so that I can't take care of it. At least handle it!

Say Mother! How's the Sunday School Class coming along? I hope you are enjoying it. For while I 'm on the subject, the only thing besides a few clothes that I managed to save was your Bible. So hang on to your classes and I'll bring you back your Bible.

Well so long, Mother dearest. Keep the old chin up, throw that beautiful gray hair of yours back and say to yourself, "No matter what happens it's for the best." I love and miss you terribly,

Your loving son,
Wendell

The last letter I wrote from Corregidor three days later and just three days before the fall Sunday, May 3rd said:

Hi! All! I'm still fine and Happy!

Dearest Mother,

Well here I am again, and you can bet your bottom dollar that I love it. For any time I can add to the appeasement of those at home I'm going to do it. Especially since mail only goes out once in every blue moon.

I'm rather happy, but I'm far from content as you can readily guess. I'm working hard trying to keep my mind occupied, but try as I may I just can't seem to keep it functioning away from the current events around here.

I do believe that I'm much better off than a lot of them and with faith constantly in "my Father in Heaven" I'll continue being better off. I know one thing, however, Mother, and that is, of all the time I've been here, and it's almost a year now, I've never once wavered in the teachings I received from you. And as events progressed I've never stopped marveling at how right you, my parents have been.

I hope that by this time you've received my three telegrams and my many letters and I also hope that you have taken everything I have written without letting it bother you too much. For as you must know we McGarrys are a very sentimental lot. And you should also know that there isn't a one that doesn't love and cherish everything about you for more than we can or ever hope to express on paper.

As much as I'd just love to fill this page with how much I have missed you, I'm afraid that it would tend to make you unhappy and make you wish that I had never come over here. Of course it's true I don't love this over here, but maybe it's where I was intended to be.

So Mother, dearest, don't fret over me too much and just remember that some day after this is all over and I've finished my dental schooling we'll agree that it was all worth it.

Mother you can change this 80 peso's at the bank for $40. Spend it on yourself. May our Father in Heaven watch over you always.

Your loving son,
Wendell

Say Dad how about giving Mother one of those big hugs and kisses for me. That goes for you too Dexter. I don't know about Sheridan, but something tells me he's been drafted. But I hope he doesn't get into this mess.

(Written down the side margin of the page) Sherman was right Dad, War is HELL!! Incidentally, you're right too.[23]

The Japanese had landed. It was Wednesday, May 5th. Topside had been overrun by the enemy. It had been courageously defended by the U.S. 4th Marines and men picked from the personnel of the three batteries of the U.S. 59th Coast Artillery. The American forces caught in the brutal cross-fire of the too-numerous Japanese troops suffered heavy casualties.[24]

An emergency defense line was set up five-hundred meters away from the mouth of the Malinta Tunnel. Every able-bodied man, whether he be a cook, ordinance man, grounded pilot, member of the 59th Coast Artillery, or the Philippine Army was pressed into service. If he could carry and operate small arms of any kind he became a defender.

The final battle for Corregidor raged throughout the night of May 5th. By 6:00 a. m. May 6th a despondent General Jonathan M. Wainwright called his exhausted battle staff to a final meeting. The enemy lines were just fifty meters away from the Malinta Tunnel entrance. When he told them he had requested permission from President Roosevelt to surrender, they tearfully but quietly concurred. The bitter decision to capitulate had been reached in order that the more than thirteen thousand lives of those still remaining on the island would be spared. A ceasefire order was issued and the weary, heartsick American defenders lay down their arms.[25]

The island fortress was on fire. The tortured, blackened, blood-soaked earth of the Rock begged for relief.

> At 10:00 a m on May 6, 1942 the American Flag was slowly brought down for the last time and a white flag of truce was raised in its place. The word that Corregidor had fallen reverberated across the globe, and the world wept.[26]

---

23. Note: Wendell was not able to say anything about the war. Anything with military significance would have been censored out. Thus the light-hearted attitude of the letter with undertones of the end looming near.
24. *Chronicle Magazine*, 6.
25. Ibid., 10.
26. Ibid.

Following is the message that was sent to President Franklin D. Roosevelt, May 6, 1942 from General Jonathan Wainwright asking for permission to surrender:

> With broken heart and head bowed in sadness but not in shame, I report to Your Excellency that today I must arrange terms for the surrender of the fortified islands of Manila Bay. . . .
>
> There is a limit of human endurance and that limit has long since been past. Without prospect of relief I feel it is my duty to my country and to my gallant troops to end this useless effusion of blood and human sacrifice. If you agree, Mr. President, please say to the nation that my troops and I have accomplished all that is humanly possible and that we have upheld the best tradition of the United States and its army. May God bless and preserve you and guide you and the nation in the effort to ultimate victory. With profound regret and with continued pride in my gallant troops I go to meet the Japanese. Goodbye, Mr. President.[27]

I don't remember what happened immediately after we were told of the surrender except the noise and concussion of the shelling could be heard and felt for quite some time. Even after the American flag had been retired and the white flag of surrender had been hoisted, the enemy continued their advance closer to the Malinta Tunnel entrance. The Japanese would not accept the surrender until the next day. [28]

In looking back over these many years, I'm sure we were all in a complete state of dazed shock and disbelief at that point in time, and we were scared. As smug Americans who had never been restricted in our activities, we had yet to realize the impact of the events that had taken place during the previous twenty-four hours. We had no idea of what the coming days, weeks and months would bring. And it was just as well we didn't.

---

27. General Wainwright's message of surrender to President Roosevelt is found in the museum on Corregidor as well as in many publications including the *Corregidor Guide Book* by Alfonso J. Aluit, Galleon Publications, Manila, Philippines, 2003.
28. *Chronicle Magazine*, 10.

Sometime after the surrender was accepted, a contingent of Japanese officers in full dress uniform covered with medals came into the hospital lateral. We had no idea what to expect. We were told to remain exactly where we were while they made an inspection. We were not to leave the hospital lateral until all of the Japanese wounded and dead had been picked up and removed from the battlefield. This would take several days.

When the Japanese officers had completed the inspection to their satisfaction we felt relieved but rather apprehensive as we went back to our hospital duties. We were still not allowed to leave the tunnel at all.

Before the surrender we would escape the sometimes close atmosphere in the tunnel laterals by going outside via the hospital entrance. Even though the air inside the tunnel was circulated and cooled somewhat by huge ventilating fans, the conditions of war, the dust and smoke, made it impossible to clear it completely. It was just good to go out of doors. At least we could have a smoke. We could rest and relax a bit for a few moments. On occasion, we would even take a blanket along and catch a few winks outside. However, the full month of April we had been under constant fire so we were totally confined to the tunnel.

One of the hospital laterals was where the nurses were quartered. This area was kept locked at all times. No one else besides nurses were allowed entrance. Another lateral was quarters for the enlisted men who worked in the tunnel. There were single bunks as well as showers for which we were very grateful. We were able to keep reasonably clean, to grab a quick shower before falling exhausted into our bunks. The other ten laterals were where the dental clinic and the one thousand bed hospital were located.

During the siege of Corregidor, all of Malinta Tunnel had become choked with hundreds of refugees, many of them from Bataan, seeking shelter from the shelling and bombing. The hospital laterals including our quarters were no exception. They were filled with wounded and dying. As a result, we would fall asleep wherever we could find an empty space where we could take the weight off from our feet, be it on the floor or in an empty chair.

During the war and after the fall when the power in other areas of the tunnel went out, the hospital remained lighted. A supplemental generator supplied the power, thus we were able to continue our care of the sick and wounded.

We were somewhat surprised a few days later when more enemy officers came into the hospital for another inspection. With them was a young Japanese man dressed in a very elaborate uniform covered with medals and decorations. He had the bearing of someone of great importance. We later learned he was a member of the Japanese Royal Family. We assumed he had come to inspect the spoils of his country's victory.

Several more days after this inspection, a group of rowdy Japanese enlisted men came noisily barging into the hospital. They were very disruptive. Wide-eyed with fright and not knowing how to react, we stood at attention. On an individual basis they approached each one of us and demanded we empty our pockets.

Our watches and rings were the first to be confiscated. Then they tore the footlockers apart rummaging through them and taking everything that suited their fancy. They eagerly gathered up the money, American and Filipino alike. They grabbed fountain pens, jewelry and all items made from the beautiful silk brocade that had been purchased to take as gifts back to the states. They took clothing and shoes as well. Miraculously, they ignored the terrified nurses and passed them by.

When I was about sixteen, my mother had finally yielded to the coaxing and begging of an insistent teenager and had given me her beautiful gold wedding band. The fact that she had gained weight and was no longer able to get it on her finger may have figured in her decision. At any rate, I had worn it on my little finger all through high school and during my college days. When I left home to go overseas, she had tearfully instructed me to bring it back to her.

I wore it continually and had managed to keep it to that point. After the fall, I was sure the Japanese would take it away from me if they were to see it. So I gave it to Lieutenant Eunice Young for safekeeping. I became friendly with this attractive army nurse as we worked together in the Malinta Tunnel Hospital. (I would have liked to have been more closely associated with her, but we adhered to army protocol which prohibited an officer from fraternizing with an enlisted man). Hoping that the enemy would pretty much leave the nurses alone, I asked her if she would keep the ring for me. She agreed to try and keep it safe until we found out what was going to happen.[29]

I was grateful she had it safely in her possession during the raid of the Japanese soldiers. A while later she returned it to me as she had been ordered to leave Corregidor with some of the other nurses. They were to be transferred to Manila where they would be kept prisoners with the civilian captives at a University called Santa Tomas.

Cutting a slit inside the waistband of my pants, I slipped the ring inside where I pinned it securely and carried it with me for the duration of my captivity, transferring it whenever I changed clothes. Many times I lovingly caressed it. Touching it seemed to give me strength and comfort. I could literally feel the love and the tenderness of my sweet mother crossing the miserable miles that separated us. Each time I felt it, I renewed my promise to live and to deliver the ring safely back into her keeping.

Sometime in 1943, after I was transferred to Cabanatuan, one of the prisoners who had been a silversmith before the war and had somehow kept his tools for engraving carved Mother's name inside the wide gold band. The tiny letters read, "Fern Hickman McGarry."

During the very difficult period in 1944 at Cabanatuan when we were all so hungry, some of the Japanese guards were supplying extra rations to those who still had barter items. I had reached the point where I was sorely tempted to trade the ring for food. I may have succumbed if it had not been for my friend Dr. McKissick who refused to let me give it up. He successfully argued I had sacrificed so much to keep it, we would find a way to survive without losing it to the enemy. Besides, I had promised to bring my mother's ring back to her.

---

29. McGarry renewed his acquaintance with Eunice Young in Manila in 1982. He reminded her about the part she had played in 1942 when she saved his mother's wedding ring from confiscation by the Japanese. Then he enjoyed a long overdue hug and a kiss on the cheek with this smiling, very pleased lady.

My wife would wear the gold band for thirty-five years before her death in 1979, and my son would place it on the third finger, left hand of his bride when he was married on September 30, 1982. Hopefully the ring, with its history, will be passed on to one of his sons some day.

THE HELL CALLED PRISON CAMP

We had been working night and day in the hospital ever since the nightmare of the surrender had taken place on May 6th. It had been several days but it seemed like an eternity. Eventually the medical personnel were allowed to go outside the Malinta Tunnel.

Evidently, the enemy wounded and dead had been gathered up and taken away. The Japanese had finally given us permission to send litter bearers out to gather up our wounded. The dead would have to wait until a later time.

I was ordered to take two litters along with eight men outside the tunnel and bring in the surviving wounded. The feelings of relief which came from being out in the open air once again were somewhat diminished as we looked around us. A smoky haze from smoldering ruins hung in suspension and the air was thick with lingering pollution. It was difficult to comprehend the total destruction that had been inflicted upon this once beautiful island. It had been completely destroyed. We continued about our tasks mechanically like toy soldiers under the command of a child.

We had not gone far from the hospital tunnel entrance when we saw several Japanese soldiers coming toward us, talking among themselves. Then they spotted us. I suppose the Red Cross on our waist bands had given us a false sense of security. I don't believe any of us were actually afraid. Apprehensive perhaps, but not exactly fearful. We stopped and were waiting for them to pass by, but this was not to be.

The Japanese soldier who seemed to be in charge began chattering orders to us in his native tongue, which we did not understand, but we knew enough to stand at attention, to wait and see what he was going to do next. Without any warning whatsoever, he slammed his fist into my jaw. The unexpected blow knocked me backward, but I stayed on my feet. Then he proceeded to pound me in the face and in the gut. When I bent over in pain, he smashed me in the mouth with his knee. He dealt blow after savage blow to my head and body. The final strike came after I stumbled and fell flat on the ground. He kicked me several times, hard, in the ribs. I gasped for breath. The searing pain was intense, like nothing I had ever felt before. The last thing I remember was the hot stinging tears coursing down my cheeks. Tears of anger, resentment, and frustration because I couldn't defend myself. And I was crying because I hurt. Then, numbing relief as I passed into the black void of unconsciousness.

That was my first beating, but it definitely would not be my last. In looking back, I'm sure it was the worst one I had to take all through prison camp, probably because it was the first of the many awful experiences that were to come. I had not only suffered physical pain but my spirit had been bruised as well.

The first bitter realization of what being a prisoner of war really meant came to me through that brutal, inhumane beating. I suddenly realized I no longer had the right to defend or to even think for myself. I had no rights at all, and this was just beginning. I pleaded, "Please, dear God give me strength. Please, don't desert me or my country during these dark hours. Be with my parents that their not knowing might be lessened."[30]

I was never able to find out exactly what happened to the squad of men who were with me that dreadful day. I didn't see any of them being beaten, but seriously doubt they had been spared.

Not knowing just how much time passed before I regained consciousness, it seemed I was awakening from an awful nightmare. Realizing I was lying in the shade on the ground, I tried to move, but was very stiff and sore. My shirt was covered with dried blood. And then I remembered. "That dirty son of

---

30. McGarry talk to senior citizens on Memorial Day, Ephraim, Utah, 1994.

a bitch!" I muttered. Shoving aside a cool, wet cloth covering swollen eyes and a lump on my forehead, I struggled to get my bearings. Hovering over me were several unfamiliar people who were wearing remnants of Marine, Army and Navy uniforms. I had no idea where I was or how I had gotten there.

"Where in the hell am I and how long have I been here?" I asked through bruised, swollen lips. I don't know who answered my question, but was told that some of them had found me, alone, not too far from the Malinta Tunnel. I was now on Bottomside in what used to be the Engineers Garage with a group of prisoners from different branches of the service.

Sometime later we were all herded into a staging area somewhere between Middleside and Bottomside. There we were divided into groups and given different details.

My group was first assigned to the burial detail. We were to pick up the dead and retrieve one of their dog tags, leaving the second one on the body for later identification. Then we carried them to the wartime cemetery on Monkey Point. Sometimes we dug the graves, other times this was done by another detail of men. This proved to be a grisly task, mentally as well as physically exhausting, draining all of our energy and our mental strength.

I heard about an incident on one of these burial details where a pair of brothers who were walking along the side of a cliff demonstrated the despair and the feelings of hopelessness that we were all beginning to feel. On the way to the cemetery, one of them broke ranks, ran to the edge of the cliff, and with the desperate cry, "I can't take any more," jumped to his death, crashing to the rocks below.

On the way back to camp, as the group neared the area where the poor guy had jumped from the cliff, the remaining sibling was heard to say something like, "What the hell! I can't go home and tell my mother what happened to him." Then he too leaped over the edge to the same fate.

There was one very strange happening on the burial detail that was repeated several times and caused all of us a lot of extra beatings. Whenever the Japanese began to pound on one or more of us, there was one American prisoner who would fall on his knees in the attitude of prayer, looking up to the sky. All the while he would be chanting something that none of us could understand. The enemy soldiers would stare in amazement at him but they never touched him. They were literally afraid of anyone they considered possessed. However, it seemed to infuriate them further and the rest of us would be beaten unmercifully.

All of us were very irritated at the guy and extremely tired of taking so much punishment because of his theatrics. We decided to put a stop to it. I was selected to give him an ultimatum. "If you ever do your little stunt again, I'll kick your head off," I threatened.

Evidently he was more afraid of our captors than he was of me. When the next opportunity came, he fell to his knees and began his stupid act. I immediately stepped forward and delivered the promised kick under the chin. He toppled over on his back, momentarily stunned, then he slowly got up and fell into ranks. The surprised Japanese herded us away to continue the detail. It never happened again.

Whenever we went on a detail, we were accompanied by several enemy enlisted men. They watched us like hawks and we were continually beaten for the slightest misstep. No matter what we did, if it didn't please them, we were severely beaten. We were slapped in the face, hit with fists, and knocked to the ground. We were kicked in the ribs and in the head, often to the point of unconsciousness.

The thing I remember most about the beatings was the hatred with which they were administered. At the time we couldn't quite understand why the Japanese literally despised us. Later on we learned that there were several reasons for their feelings of utter contempt.

First, a good share of these soldiers were hard-core killers. They had fought in Malaysia, Singapore, and China. Killing was second nature to them. I 'm sure many of them had been away from family and home for years. Killing was all that they had known for a long time; it had become a way of life. Revenge and hatred filled their very souls and we were the recipients of those deep-seated emotions.

Second, we were the reason they were still away from home. The whole Philippine campaign and surrender was supposed to have been short and easy to accomplish, and finished much sooner than it actually happened. It lasted months longer, and the expenditure of time, Japanese resources, and lives had been extremely expensive.[31]

Third, and perhaps the strongest reason for the contempt they had for us, was that in their native culture it was an absolute act of cowardice for a soldier to surrender and become a prisoner of war. They were taught there was honor in death. They were also taught it was a disgrace to one's family and to the emperor to surrender. It was much more courageous to die, even at their own hands. They considered us cowards of the worst kind.

When I left the Malinta Tunnel, I had the clothes on my back and the shoes on my feet. That was all except a few medical supplies and my mother's little Bible, which were in my pockets. Mom's wedding ring was still safely pinned inside the band on my pants.

Everyone was in the same boat, so we became scavengers. We picked up clothing, shoes, and anything else scattered about that we could see a use for and we carried the booty back to our quarters.

Finally, the burial details came to an end. We were then given a detail to clean up the barracks on Middleside. They had been partially destroyed in the twenty-seven days of shelling and bombing. However, there was a section where lots of repair and cleaning up of debris could be made into livable quarters for the Japanese soldiers.

It was during this detail that a really funny thing happened. When I remember it, I still laugh. We had pretty much finished with the cleaning detail when one of the guys discovered a store room with bags of rice in it. The Japanese soldiers who were watch-dogging the detail were outside on the shady side of the building, probably sleeping. The rice looked clean and we imagined eating all we wanted of whole cooked rice instead of the mushy, gooey concoction of lugao,[32] which was always filled with pieces of debris and peppered with huge black flies. We

---

31. *Chronicle Magazine*, 6.
32. Lugao is the Filipino name for white rice which was boiled in water for many hours without salt to a thick, sticky consistency and served for the evening meal, portions too small to satisfy hunger and mostly lacking in nutrition.

decided to tie the bottom of our pant legs tightly around our ankles with pieces of twine. We could then put a cup or two of rice inside. We tried it, and unless you knew it was there, it wouldn't even be noticed.

I don't remember how many guys were on the detail, but most of us had successfully completed the operation with rice in our trousers when the Japanese soldier yelled that we were ready to go back to our quarters. With the exception of one short guy who was noted for his greediness, we all walked outside. When he came out of the barracks, he was waddling like a duck. He had loaded both of his pant legs with rice. They looked like elongated, partially inflated balloons and they were heavy. He couldn't get his legs together and he looked hilarious. The Americans snickered, then laughed outright. The Japanese soldiers looked at him quizzically and the inevitable happened. The strings around his ankles came untied. The rice poured out into piles on the ground. All of us laughed hysterically. But the Japanese saw no humor whatsoever in the whole incident. Each of us was made to untie the strings around our pant legs and let the rice out. Then we cleaned up the mess, all the while being pummeled, whacked, and otherwise soundly beaten.

Our punishment continued, but even as we stood at attention for several hours in the blazing sun, occasionally someone would attempt to stifle a chuckle and we would all join in. When the funny incident was retold many times, the result was always the same, a good enjoyable belly laugh. For a few moments we could all forget our miserable circumstances and just be Americans again, not POWs.

After the barracks cleaning details were finished, my group was assigned to the scrap metal detail. This was a very hot, unpleasant, grueling task to say the least. It was extremely hard work picking up the blackened scrap metal with bare hands, loading it on to vehicles and taking it to the docks where we carried it into the holds of tramp steamers.

We rotated the jobs of loading the heavy metal into the bowels of the ships as the temperature in the oppressive atmosphere of the hold hovered around one hundred twenty degrees. Inside, we worked organizing the scrap and piling it up for transport.

The hoards of huge, ugly cockroaches which covered the floor crunched into a slimy foothold and added to the misery of the furnace-like heat. It was impossible to tolerate the extremely uncomfortable temperature for more than a few minutes without passing out. I came close several times.

The Japanese guards on these details were ruthless. They would tear into one of the prisoners who didn't pick up the right piece of scrap or who hesitated when placing it on the truck. We committed infractions without even realizing it. We couldn't do anything right in their eyes. We not only endured the hard work, the heat, and the beatings, but the stress and uncertainty of not knowing who would be next. It was one hell of a detail and it lasted much longer than I care to remember. There would be more of these uncomfortable situations to come, many more.

By the time the hot and muggy 4th of July, 1942 arrived, we had been prisoners of the Japanese for almost two months. At this time I was still with the guys at the Engineers Garage on Bottomside where I had been taken soon after the surrender. The ensuing time had been difficult, to say the least. We had been beaten unmercifully without rhyme or reason. We had been humiliated and abused emotionally as well as physically. The degradation and cruelty of slavery had injured our spirits as well as our bodies.

Over the more than sixty years since all of these awful experiences were an integral part of my life, I have tried with some success to mentally block out the really traumatic times. I have tried to remember the good, the humorous times and the people who were involved. There were a few. I haven't been able to fully forget some of the incidences of cruelty and injustice, nor have I been able to completely forgive the perpetrators. But I do remember an especially interesting beating I received at the hand of a young, larger than usual Japanese soldier.

I don't remember what the circumstances were that preceded the incident, but I do remember this guy, rather than exhibiting anger or hatred, was actually enjoying hurting me. Every time he hit me with such force I would fall on my behind, I would swear at him. Then I would struggle to my feet only to be punched again and find myself in the dirt.

I suddenly realized he understood what I was saying, and when I confronted him with, "You-son-of-a-bitch, you understand English don't you?" He replied in flawless English, "Yes, I lived in California. I studied at UCLA."

That ended the beating. He gave me no explanation as to why he was fighting with the Japanese army and I didn't ask. Then he offered me a cigarette and we sat down. As we smoked, we came to the consensus that we were each doing our duty, whatever it was, that our countries expected of us. We were both victims of circumstances over which we had no control. He was one of the conquerors and I was one of the conquered. I decided it was an interesting observation on the part of both of us, and it did give me a bit more rationalization for and understanding of the harsh treatment we were receiving.

We were all totally surprised, but cautiously optimistic when the Japanese commanding officer (CO) sent out a directive that the 4th of July had been declared a holiday and there would be no work for any of us. We were instead to be indulged in our national pastime, a baseball game. The Japanese soldiers were to compete against the Americans. The two teams were issued balls, bats and even some gloves that came from who knew where? The game was to be played on the repaired parade ground. Evidently the Japanese considered baseball their national pastime as well. One of their best players was a sergeant who seemed to enjoy being a cut above the rest of the players.

Several innings were played without incident. Then the Japanese non-com (non-commissioned officer) came up to bat. The American pitcher fired a fast ball across home-plate. The resounding crack of the bat as it connected with the ball echoed across the parade ground. A line drive close to first base was snagged in an American glove. The more-than-pleased grin on the face of the Jap sergeant showed he was safe on first.

The pitcher snapped the ball smartly into his glove several times as he eyeballed the over-anxious sergeant who was stretching his body toward second base, all the while keeping his toe on the first base marker and his eye on the pitcher. After a partial wind-up, looking as if he intended to throw the ball to the waiting batter, the pitcher turned and ambled slowly over to the first base. He whispered something into the first-baseman's ear. In the process he pressed the ball deep into the American player's mitt, then he strolled leisurely back to the mound.

Shouts of encouragement to the pitcher, the batter, and the potential runner stirred the hot, humid air. The pitcher wound up as he prepared for a mighty pitch across home plate. As the hapless sergeant left the safety of first base and eagerly dug his heels into the dirt for a dash to second base, the player at first reached out with his hand and tagged him with the ball.

A split second of stunned silence followed the umpire's dramatic, "Out!" Then came the uproarious laughter and whistles from the Americans. They were joined by grins, snickers, then peals of laughter from the Japanese teammates. Of course, the bewildered sergeant took a second to realize what had happened, then he began venting his displeasure and frustrated anger on the nearest person. He meted out insults and blows to anyone he could catch, Japanese and American alike, who were all dashing around trying to avoid him. Needless to say, that was the end of the 4th of July baseball game.

I did not play in the game, but I had been one of the delighted spectators who had the pleasure of witnessing the humiliation of a Japanese non-com. And I reaped my reward the next day along with everyone else. We were awakened early and put to work, with no consideration, little rest and short rations. Somehow, the humor of the whole thing faded a bit as the very long work day seemed doomed to go on forever.

I was still quartered in the large garage that had been used by the Engineers Unit where their equipment was stored and repaired before the war. Even though it had been badly damaged during the siege, it had been sufficiently repaired and would serve as housing for our group until July 24th. Occasionally I would be sent to the tunnel on a detail.

I remember a lateral just off the main tunnel, not sure just where, but each time I passed this area I would look at a huge safe that was standing inside. It was a big one, taller than I was. I wondered what was in it. On one trip to the tunnel, I saw a detail of Americans rummaging through piles of papers near the big old safe. My curiosity got the best of me and I asked what they were doing. They told me the safe had been forced open and its contents were scattered about.

Later I learned that in the process of cleaning the safe out, the guys had discovered another little safe in the bottom and clear to the back of the big one. The door had probably been forced open as well. Inside was the Filipino First Lady, Mrs. Quezon's, jewelry. Evidently with the rapid departure of the President and his family from the Malinta Tunnel, the jewelry had simply been forgotten.

I saw some of it and I wished there was a way I could get a pair of the diamond earrings for my mother. They were really exquisite but that was wistful thinking as I had nothing of value to trade. However, the POWs who found the cache had devised a way to keep some of the jewelry. They bribed the Japanese guard. After he had gotten several pieces for himself, he allowed the Americans to keep the rest of it to sell or trade for things they wanted.

Several of the guys decided they would pierce their ears and wear some of Mrs. Quezon's earrings just so they would know who each other was after the war. Stupid idea. The Japanese guard changed and the new guard was not so easily swayed. In fact, when he saw the earrings in the soldier's ears he proceeded to jerk them out, painfully tearing their ear lobes. I imagine the rest of the jewelry was taken by the new guard.

On the south side of the main tunnel the first lateral from the east entrance served as pre-war headquarters of the Harbor Defense Command under General George Moore. The fourth lateral on the same side extended into a group of twelve more laterals which were used as the quartermaster supply storage.[33]

It was the middle of July of 1942 and we had been prisoners for almost two and one half months. During that time, it was to this storage unit that some of us had been sent on several details. Food was stored there that most of us thought we would never get to see again, let alone get to taste. Canned goods we had not dreamed existed anywhere on the island were there. After several weeks the same diet of rice and dried fish every day

---

33. Information found in the museum on Corregidor, 2006.

had become very tiresome. A variety of anything else would be welcome, so four of us decided to get some of it, no matter what.

All we needed was a note from someone in authority. We counted on the fact that the Japanese were not well versed in the written English language. I don't remember who it was that wrote the note which we presented to the guard at the tunnel entrance, but he let us in without question. Each of us grabbed a case of something from the shelves and hurriedly carried it out of the tunnel. When we arrived back at the Engineer's Garage, we distributed the contraband to our hungry counterparts until it was all gone. I think we enjoyed it much more because of having fooled the Japanese guard so easily—or so we thought.

Just because he couldn't read English did not make the guard stupid. I'm sure he had gone to his superior officer after the raid on the supply room and told him of the episode with these brazen Americans.

The whole incident had proven to be so successful and fun for the guys they decided to do it again. I tried to discourage them with the idea that the Japanese would fall for it once, but they would be wise to the scheme and the prisoners would get caught if they tried it again, but to no avail. They presented the note to the guard again, this time without me, and as I had predicted, they got caught and were severely punished.

In the process they were forced to rat on me and I was marched back to the tunnel to receive my punishment. There was an American prisoner named Sergeant Provoo[34] present who spoke fluent Japanese and was acting as interpreter. For his services in collaborating with the enemy, he received sufficient food, good treatment, and avoided the beatings the rest of us endured. He seemed to enjoy seeing me being severely punished. I hated Provoo even more than the Japanese soldier who was giving me the beating!

That ended the raids on the supply room.

---

34. According to a report in the *Salt Lake Tribune* newspaper in September 1945, Sergeant Provoo was arrested by the FBI and charged with treason in Federal Court.

– 6 –

FORT FRANK CARABAO ISLAND

Beatings had become commonplace, each one seeming to outdo the others. God became all important to me. I asked to overcome these ordeals and above all to try and suffer these oppressions with honor that my God, my country, and my parents could understand. My God was kind to me. For every detail was not always hell. Fort Frank was one of these.[35]

It was July 24th, marking a little more than my first two months in captivity, and I was tired. I was sick and tired of the brutal treatment all of us had endured at the hands of our Japanese captors. We had been beaten with "vitamin sticks," which could be anything from heavy clubs to pieces of bamboo that had been split length-wise several times. These were razor sharp and would lacerate the skin and flesh, leaving gaping, bleeding wounds wherever they inflicted their damage.

Dozens of huge, black blow flies would instantly smell the fresh blood and settle in to lay their eggs. We continued to work until unable to endure the agony any longer. When we would stop and try to get rid of the flies we were beaten again. It was brutal.

The only relief came when we were back at the Engineers' Garage and could apply silver nitrate crystals to the wounds. I had brought the nitrate from the Malinta Tunnel Hospital. It sterilized the wound, stopped the bleeding, and killed the

---

35. McGarry talk, Ephraim, 1994.

emerging maggots. The stinging sensation was excruciating but it did the trick, leaving ugly black stains along the length of the cuts.

We had also been kicked with heavy boots, slapped, spit upon, and otherwise grossly humiliated.

> All hell began with the hours of Russian Roulette, flinching every time the trigger hit the cylinder, not daring to move because of their bayonets and the guards who laughed with each click and roared when the chamber was full.[36]

All too often we had become human pawns in the sometimes deadly but always nerve wracking mental and emotional torture of the game in which our Jap captors took such gross pleasure.

I especially abhorred the fact that all of our freedom was gone and with it every bit of human dignity and self respect. We were no longer worth anything. We had become mere numbers with less status than the mongrel dogs roaming Corregidor Island. Our virtual existence was only attributed to the slave labor we provided. We belonged to the Japanese body and soul. We were theirs to do with as they saw fit. We were worked to utter exhaustion, picking up scrap metal and burying the dead no matter what our physical condition might be. We worked with high temperatures, symptoms of Dengue fever, or Malaria. We had been forced to go on details while suffering the pain of dysentery and the indignities of not being allowed to relieve ourselves, wallowing like swine in our own filth until the work day came to an end.

> Gratefully, we were staying near the waterfront where we were allowed to bathe and wash our clothing after our days work. We were fed anything our captors chose to feed us, or we were fed nothing. We were abused at their slightest whim and we were theirs to do away with at any time they desired.[37]

In this frame of mind I totally ignored the hard and fast rule of the "Old Army," which was not to volunteer for anything.

---

36. Mother's Bible. Wendell's mother sent her bible with him when he went to war. He made notes in the margins throughout his years of captivity. All references to Mother's Bible are from this source.
37. McGarry tak to Senior Citizen's, 1994.

When the opportunity presented itself for the first voluntary detail that came along, I signed up. I was sure nothing could be worse than the situation I found myself in for what seemed an eternity, even though it was a mere two month's time. Working long hard hours in the unrelenting heat, eating but never being full, sleeping but never being rested, I had just about reached the end of my rope.

It was rumored that this detail was leaving Corregidor for an unknown destination. There were eleven other Americans besides me when we boarded the little supply boat. We were transported to Fort Frank located on Carabao Island. This island was one of the smaller giant boulders which made up the four fortified islands in the huge Manila Bay. It was an R and R (Rest and Recreation) Camp for the Japanese soldiers. We were to be their slaves and to provide whatever physical comforts they desired.

When we arrived at the dock on Carabao Island the tide was in and we were able to step from the boat onto it. We carried the supplies that came with us up a series of steep steps which wound around the hill to the flat top to the storage area kitchen. Hope surged through my heart. Perhaps this experience would be one to remember with less bitterness than the one on Corregidor had been. Time would tell.

Captain Horiuchi, the Japanese officer in charge of Fort Frank, was a well-educated, good-looking young man about my size. He spoke fairly good English and he treated us with a degree of respect. He did not approve of the harsh treatment that was meted out by some of his enlisted men. At one time there was a new group of enemy soldiers who came to the island for R and R and brought with them American prisoners. I recognized one of them as a guy I had known on Corregidor. When they were beating him unmercifully, I wanted Horiuchi to intervene, but he discouraged me with the statement, "These are bad men; they will kill you."

I did witness a beating while on Fort Frank that, in spite of the hurt that was eventually inflicted upon a fellow soldier, was downright funny.

There was this young, gangly, six-feet-six-inch-tall American who had been appropriately nicknamed "Two-Meters." One day a small Japanese soldier became very angry with Two-Meters for some long since forgotten reason and proceeded to give him a beating. The favorite place to hit a prisoner was always in the face. Because of the difference in their height, the soldier could not reach his victim's face. So he found a box and climbed up on it that he might reach his target. The only problem then was in order to avoid being struck in the face, Two-Meters would continually dodge the blows, which threw the Japanese soldier off balance and he would fall from the box. Each time that this happened, he would climb back and try in vain to hit his towering victim.

Finally the now livid soldier found a stick, climbed back up on the box, and scored a blow or two. After several more misses which resulted in a fall each time, he enlisted the help of several other guards and eventually succeeded in beating the unfortunate Two Meters into submission. Still seething with rage and embarrassment, he strode indignantly away. The delighted laughter from all of the spectators may have contributed to the batter's utter humiliation.

One day shortly after our arrival at Fort Frank, an American submarine lurking in the China Sea nearby fired a torpedo which hit the island and exploded. It created quite a stir among the Japanese. They were certain that the Americans were coming. We were excited as well until several Japanese fighter planes flew overhead. Then we knew that it was just a fluke.

One of our first duties was to find and stack all of the lumber that we could find from the destroyed buildings. The captain also told us to find all of the "needles" we could and bring them to him. Puzzled, we looked through our meager belongings and came up with a few. When we showed him what we had found, he became very angry and sent us away.

He later came to us and apologized for his mistake. What he wanted were "nails" to aid in the construction of housing for the Japanese and for us. He served us tea and rice cakes along with the humble apology. This was unheard of and something that we had never hoped to see while in captivity.

We constructed a building out of salvaged materials with a small private room for Captain Horiuchi. The rest of the building was quarters for his men and on the other side of a partition was where the twelve Americans slept. It was rather small, cramped and definitely crude but it provided shelter from the wind and the rain.

We were fed much better rations at Fort Frank than when we were on Corregidor. We ate what the Japanese ate. They would throw hand grenades into the ocean and we would swim out with floating reed baskets and harvest the fish that had been killed in the explosion. I also remember seeing a giant turtle that swam on a consistent basis around the island. Grenades were tossed in her direction but we were never able to enjoy the turtle soup we had envisioned.

> At cooking we were a flop, mostly because at that point in time our knowledge of Japanese was practically nil. So we were manhandled quite often over it. Beatings tend to make you understand faster and we learned more as we worked.[38]

As I said earlier, we were allowed to bathe regularly and to wash our clothes. Conditions were much improved. These were totally new experiences for us as prisoners. In the process, my body was healing and the pain in my spirit had eased. This would be the only time in my captivity I was not always hungry.

These Japanese soldiers were very different from the ones who had brutalized us on Corregidor. They were mostly young men. They did not seem to be obsessed with hatred for us as Americans. It didn't seem to matter to them that we had surrendered. They delighted in sporting events to keep them entertained and we were often included.

I had become quite friendly with several of them. There was one enlisted man in particular I really liked. I thought I would never forget his name, but time has taken its toll on my memory. I'm not sure, but I think it was Yusuki. He was a fun-loving sort of guy and he was always looking for someone to wrestle with him.

I remember one day in particular when he challenged me to a wrestling match. We were about the same size and after

---

38. Ibid.

being on Fort Frank for a couple of months, I had regained much of my physical strength. So I accepted the challenge. We struggled for a time hand-to-hand in fairly even opposition amid shouts of encouragement from the American and the Japanese bystanders. Breath was coming rapidly and we were sweating profusely, however, we both stayed on our feet. After a few minutes of grappling back and forth, I got in a lucky move and my opponent crashed to the earth with me on top of him, grimacing and grunting to stay there.

Cheers and jeers filled the air. The noise apparently attracted the attention of a Japanese officer who strode quickly over to where we were writhing in the dust. He grabbed me by the belt and jerked me to my feet. He slapped me across the face several times. Then with his fist he struck a blow to my head and knocked me down, all the while chattering in his broken English that an American prisoner should not beat up on a Japanese soldier. Then he turned and marched away muttering to himself.

My wrestling opponent helped me to my feet and apologized for the beating I had taken. His sympathy and sincere apology made me hurt a little less. And he accepted defeat.

In the "Old Army" it seemed that there were nearly always one or two boys from the Ozark Mountains in every outfit, and they were very proficient in the art of still construction and the production of white lightning, a very potent liquor usually made from corn. We considered ourselves lucky to have one of these mountain boys in our group of twelve Americans. Upon inquiry he assured us of his expertise in building a still and in the production of an alcoholic beverage. Perhaps not as potent as white lightning, but the resulting rice wine would give us the effective results we wanted. We all helped scrounge up the necessary items to equip the still. We gave him the required rations of rice and then we waited.

I don't remember just how long it took for the fermenting process to take place, but soon the moment of truth arrived. We made arrangements to sample the resulting rice wine on one of the days the supply boat was not expected. We would have plenty of leisure time to enjoy the results at the connoisseur's party.

After our first sampling of the colorless, slightly cloudy liquid, we had just begun to enjoy the glow that was taking effect when Murphy's Law took over and reality set in. We were told the supply boat had docked and we were to go down and unload it. Now. It was mid-afternoon and it was hotter than hell but we had no choice. We would unload the boat even if we were already loaded.

The hike down the steps to the wharf was uneventful even though I was feeling slightly giddy and light-headed. We had just reached the dock and had begun to unload the supply boat when someone said, "Sure is getting dark; the sun must have gone behind a cloud." I looked around and for a fleeting moment the sun was shining brightly; then it began to get really dark. One by one the darkness closed in upon us and we were all blind as bats. The damn rice wine had cast its magic spell on us and we couldn't see anything!

I couldn't believe what was happening. Here we were in a foreign land, thousands of miles from home, prisoners of the Japanese and we were stone-blind for perhaps the rest of our lives. The thought was terrifying.

Because we couldn't tell where the end of the dock was, we dropped to our knees and began crawling gingerly away from the edge, carefully feeling with our hands. We were shouting, calling to each other in an attempt to avoid falling into the water. With one another's help and directions, we found the steps and began to crawl, still on our hands and knees, up to the top of the island. The Japanese watched the drama unfold in stunned silence. They were really afraid of any strange or unnatural behavior, and these actions certainly fit into the strange category!

We finally reached the top of the steps, made our way to our quarters, and fell onto our beds. There we stayed until morning, sleeping as if we were dead.

As the morning sun shone brightly outside, I was awakened by the sounds of the agitated Japanese whispering and peering intently through the windows at us to make sure we were indeed still alive. And then someone shouted, "I can see, I can see!" We could all see again. We were ecstatic. The joyful demonstration once again briefly stunned our captors. They even smiled.

Very soon we were soundly reprimanded by Captain Horiuchi. We decided then and there the rice wine experience need not be repeated, at least not now.

I am sure the drastic effects the wine had on us was because none of us had even tasted anything alcoholic for so long. Our bodies reacted acutely and violently to the stimulant, coupled with the intense heat of the day, thus causing the temporary blindness. Thank the good Lord it was temporary!

Captain Horiuchi had been given the opportunity to advance to the rank of major, but he needed math, geometry, and trigonometry to meet the qualification of the advancement. Since I was the only former college student, it fell to me to be his tutor. He learned quickly and was soon proficient in all of the subjects. In the process I believe we became friends. We treated each other with respect and I learned to enjoy him.

The twelve of us had become his Americans. He had even given us Japanese names. Mine was Komosa. I only remember one other name, Omasa. My time on Fort Frank with Major Horiuchi was absolutely the best time of my nearly three years of captivity. He protected us and always gave us special treatment.

I remember just one of the other eleven Americans with whom I spent so much time on Fort Frank. He was Carl Lindon, from Friendship, Wisconsin. After returning home we corresponded at Christmastime every year until his death.

After the fall of Corregidor, the Japanese had appointed an American Major Lothrup to be in charge of all of the American captives in the fortified islands. His work was subject to the Japanese commander. Lothrup was a disagreeable fellow, and we all agreed he was a little crazy. He believed that the Americans could become armed with the weapons that were scrounged up after the fighting ceased and could successfully revolt. His theory was that it was possible for us to make our escape on a yacht which had belonged to Manuel L. Quezon, the Filipino President. It was this insane idea and his stupid actions on one occasion that could have easily gotten me killed.

Because I had been a medic in the Malinta Tunnel Hospital

before the fall of Corregidor, I had been appointed to the medical duties on Fort Frank. One day I was sent back to Corregidor aboard the supply boat to obtain medical supplies as well as rice flour and other items. Dr. Emil Merkle was my physician contact on Corregidor and he regularly supplied me with meds, as well as his expertise on any problem I encountered. I was always glad to visit with this good friend with whom I kept in contact after the war. He died at age ninety-one in the year 2000 in Hayden, Idaho.

The supplies had been loaded aboard the little boat and I was informed that several of the bags of flour contained weapons and ammunition, which didn't particularly bother me until several Japanese soldiers came aboard. On the short trip back to Fort Frank, the soldiers noticed an open bag of rice flour. They thrust their hands into it and let the finely ground grain filter through their fingers, all the while making comments on its merits. I became extremely nervous. Walking to the stern of the boat I made the fool-hardy decision to jump overboard if one of the weapons was found. I'm not sure what would have happened in that event except I would not have been in the boat to reap the consequences. Luckily, the guns were buried deep enough into the bags that they were not discovered.

As I said, Major Lothrup was not only disagreeable but extremely jealous of anyone who he perceived in any way trying to usurp his power. He liked to be in charge and make the decisions. He was totally nuts.

When he discovered what was going on with Captain Horiuchi's twelve Americans, Major Lothrop was furious. He disagreed with the work details and the treatment given to these Americans. He waited for his opportunity to remedy the situation.

It was now February 15, 1943 and our almost seven months on Fort Frank was about to come to an end.[39] Captain Horiuchi left Carabao Island to take his examinations for the promotion. When Major Lothrup heard he was gone, he immediately rounded up the twelve Americans and we were all sent back

---

39. Notes from mother's Bible.

to Corregidor. Our quarters were makeshift barracks near the Power Plant on Bottomside.

When the boat landed at Bottomside and we went ashore, the Major immediately made us stand at attention. He was an arrogant little bastard in his clean uniform and shiny leather boots that came almost to his knees. He proceeded to give us orders at the rate of a mile a minute. In addition, we were read the riot act as to how we would behave and anything else he could think of to lecture us about. We appeared to listen intently to his tirade, but in reality we were ignoring him and everything he said. Then one of the twelve Americans said something that sent him into a screaming fit. He remarked, "And Hitler was only a corporal." It was all that the rest of us could do to keep from laughing our heads off.

We were given the most disgusting details—garbage details, cleaning out the latrines, and anything else Major Lothrup could think of to make us pay miserably for the treatment we received from Captain Horiuchi. He was getting to us and we hated every minute we spent doing the dirty work. Even more so, we dreaded the times the major would come around to do his rigid inspections and dump his harsh criticism on us. We became targets for all of the "Old Army" jargon at his disposal which he frequently spewed out.

Then one day the miracle we prayed for occurred. We were in the process of cleaning out a particularly filthy, vile latrine when a Japanese officer who was being driven around the area shouted for his driver to stop. The new Major Horiuchi jumped from his vehicle, strode over to us, and with great consternation and scorn declared emphatically, "His Americans would not do that kind of work!"

Once again we became the objects of his affection and were invited to his quarters where we were allowed to bathe and wash our filthy clothes. He gave us long pieces of material (G strings) that went around our waist, through the crotch, and threaded under the waist band in front to cover our naked bodies while our clothes dried. Then we were once again treated to rice cakes and tea.

Major Lothrup was enraged when he found out Major Horiuchi had found his twelve Americans and was again giving us the royal treatment. He did everything he could to keep us on details where Major Horiuchi could not find us, but it still happened on isolated occasions when he ran across us and Lothrup was powerless to stop it. We were delighted whenever we were invited to Major Horiuchi's quarters where we totally enjoyed his company and the refreshments.

I remember one more detail at the time that wasn't so bad. In fact it proved to be quite pleasant with one exception. There was an ice plant in connection with the power plant. Several of us were given the responsibility to deliver ice to the Japanese Officer's quarters. In the hot, humid atmosphere of Corregidor it was a true luxury.

The ice was made in blocks about two to three feet wide, two feet high and eighteen inches thick. Each one weighed close to one hundred pounds. We would pick the big blocks up with tongs, place them on a truck and drive to the officer's quarters. With the aid of ice picks, they would be broken into quarters and deposited into ice boxes which were precursors to refrigerators.

One day as we were preparing to make a delivery, a couple of us had picked up one of the heavy, slippery blocks. We were lifting it up to load on to the truck when it slid out of the tongs and landed on the ground. The block teetered back and forth and before I could get my right foot completely out of the way, it crashed onto it, mashing my big toe.

I went to the infirmary where Dr. Merkle was working. He cleansed the rapidly swelling, bruised toe and lifted off the nail. Then he bandaged it with this statement "You won't have to ever worry about getting an ingrown toenail." Wrong! Years later I did just that, suffered a painful ingrown toenail. In addition, it remained tender the rest of my life. Even now, I sleep winter and summer with that foot sticking out from underneath the covers.

When I went into the army, my Mother gave me her little Bible. Through the five months of intense fighting and the eventual fall of Corregidor, my time on Fort Frank and back to the Rock, I had been able to hang on to it. I used it to write notes to her, sometimes only a few words, in the margins and across the top of the pages. I also wrote a few dates and events which helped me keep track of the time and places when I was transferred. One notation says, "On June 8, 1943 the boys from Topside have been sent to Manila and to the Bilibid Prison."[40]

On June 30, 1943 I was transferred to Bilibid Prison in Manila on Luzon Island. I never saw Major Horiuchi or any of "his Americans" again, but I will always cherish the memory of the time I spent on Fort Frank. I will remember a time when my bruised and battered body healed, when the bitterness and hatred which built up in my soul after suffering the brutality on Corregidor was allowed to fade away. This miracle of healing occurred because of the humane treatment, the kindness, and respect I received from a Japanese officer who was not only my friend, but who was truly "a scholar and a gentleman."

After the Americans had retaken Corregidor in 1945, I heard through the grapevine that all of the Japanese officers on Corregidor had been killed during the final battle. My assumption is that Major Horiuchi suffered the same fate.

---

40. Notes from Mother's Bible.

PHOTOGRAPHS & DOCUMENTS

Beach at Lingayan Gulf (1982)

Santa Tomas University Women and Civilian POW Camp (1982)

*This group of XPOWs were all held captive at Cabanatuan
between 1942 and 1945. They are standing in front of the
monument at the present day prison campsite.
This photo was taken while on tour in 1982.*

XPOWs and wives at Cabanatuan water tank site monument 1982.

IT'S A BIRD! IT'S A PLANE, AN AMERICAN PLANE!

Superman would not have been so welcome! Drawing by artist
Ben Steele, a Montana born cowboy who is an XPOW. He is
a survivor of the Bataan Death March, a former prisoner at
Camp O'Donnell, Bilibid Prison, Cabanatuan Prison and
in 1944 he was shipped to Japan to work in the coal mines
on Honshu Island. He was liberated by American troops in 1945.
Ben will be 97 years old in 2013. He and his wife Shirley live in
Billings, Montana where he still draws and paints. Wendell
and Ben met at Sandpoint, ID in 1990. They immediately became
dear friends. They loved and understood each other completely.

Dr. Wendell H. McGarry and Donna MacKay McGarry (1960)

Dr. Wendell H. McGarry and Gwen A. Jacobson McGarry (1981)

Manila Hotel Lobby (1982)

President Marco's Palace (1982)

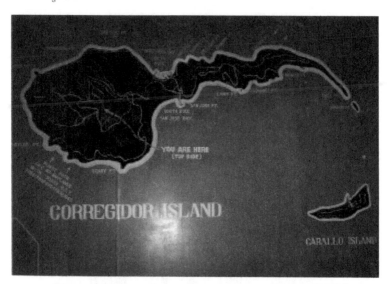

Photo of a map at the museum on Corregidor, PI (2006)

View of Corregidor from boat coming from Manila (2006)

Fern Ellen Hickman McGarry and Sheridan McGarry (1958)
Wendell's Parents

Wendell with his brothers and sisters (youngest to oldest 1981) Dexter,
Sheridan, LaRue, Wendell, Fern, Cullen, Vera, Chauncy, Derrell

Colonel Jesus Villamore: Filipino Flying Ace

Brigadier General George Moore:
Wendell's Commanding Officer on Corregidor

American Military Cemetery, Manila, PI (May 1982)

Wendell and Colonel Eunice Young

North Entrance: An interesting tourist attraction

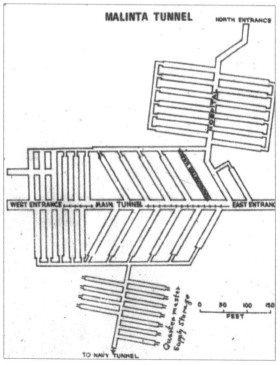

Main tunnel and lateral layout.

Wendell in the main Malinta Tunnel (1982)

Wendell at the entrance to the hospital tunnel (1982)

Former POWs at Bilibid Prison (1998)
Merrill Lee, Walter Pancratz, Wendell McGarry, Magnor Peterson

Filipino Prisoners inside Bilibid Prison (1998)

Corregidor as a tourist destination: green and beautiful. (2006)

The Pacific War Memorial on Corregidor (2006)

SALT LAKE CITY, UTAH, SATURD.

He's Termed a 'Male Tokyo Rose'

Former U. S. army sergeant John David Provoo, right, wears handcuffs as he leaves court in N. Y. Friday with a U. S. marshal. He was arrested by F B I and charged with treason helping Japanese.

FBI Charges Former G. I. With Treason

NEW YORK, Sept. 2 (UP)—Federal Bureau of Investigation agents Friday arrested on a treason charge a former U. S. army sergeant accused of "assisting" the Japanese occupation of Corregidor and taking part in Tokyo propaganda broadcasts beamed to American troops during World War II.

Described as "a male Tokyo Rose," John David Provoo, 33, native born resident of San Francisco, Cal., was seized on Governor's Island immediately after his discharge from the army upon completion of a regular term of enlistment.

Held Without Bail

Provoo was arraigned before U. S. Commissioner Edward McDonald and held without bail pending a hearing Sept. 5. He was immediately removed to the federal house of detention.

U. S. Atty. John F. X. McGohey charged that Provoo, who is of German ancestry, was captured by the Japanese when they won Corregidor on May 6, 1941. At the time Provoo was attached to the headquarters of the U. S. army in the Philippines.

McGohey charged that the lean, six-foot-two Californian, began collaborating with the Japanese army immediately after the fall of "the rock" and later was taken to Tokyo where he lived in comparative comfort with a group of about 50 American, Dutch, Australian and British collaborators who broadcast for the Japanese.

'Numerous Acts'

McGohey said that Provoo not only participated in preparing radio programs and performed on them in broadcasts from Tokyo to U. S. troops, but that he also "did perform numerous acts to assist the imperial Japanese army in the occupation of Corregidor."

On McGohey's request McDonald ordered Provoo held without bail until next week during which time Provoo will be able to obtain an attorney and to apply to federal district court for bail.

Salt Lake Tribune, September 2, 1945

MILITARY PRISON CAMP NO. 2 OF THE PHILIPPINE ISLANDS, MANILA, P.I.

January 9, 1945.

MEMORANDUM FOR ALL WARD SURGEONS AND BUILDING LEADERS:

1. The following memorandum will be read to all personnel in your building at evening Yenko this date and then posted on Bulletin Boards:

"Patients from Wards 1, 2, and 3 this morning were seen to be eating garbage that had been designated for the pigs. This trash is contaminated and may cause a fatal type of food poisoning.

All personnel are forbidden from handling or eating garbage at any time.

WARREN A. WILSON,
Major, M.C., U.S. Army,
Senior Medical Officer.

Ward-------

Memorandum on bulletin board at Bilibid

THE WHITE HOUSE
WASHINGTON

TO MEMBERS OF UNITED STATES ARMED FORCES LIBERATED
IN THE PHILIPPINE ISLANDS:

It gives me special pleasure to welcome you back to your native shores, and to express, on behalf of the people of the United States, the joy we feel at your deliverance from the hands of the enemy. It is a source of profound satisfaction that our efforts to accomplish your return have been successful.

You have fought valiantly in foreign lands and have suffered greatly. As your Commander in Chief, I take pride in your past achievements and express the thanks of a grateful Nation for your services in combat and your steadfastness while a prisoner of war.

May God grant each of you happiness and an early return to health.

Franklin D. Roosevelt

Letter from President Roosevelt

Return to Salt Lake City March 26, 1945

Joyce (1945)

7

INTO UNCHARTED TERRITORY—AGAIN

After my return to Corregidor from Fort Frank, I was housed near the power plant on Bottomside close to the docks. It was an excellent position from which to greet the Navy divers as they returned from Manila and the Bilibid prison. These lucky guys were commandeered by the Japanese to dive into Manila Bay and retrieve the silver coins and bars stored in the Malinta tunnel before the fall of Corregidor. The Americans dumped them into the Manila Bay when word came that the landing of the Japanese made surrender inevitable. The gold bars and coins were removed earlier aboard submarines.

The Navy divers looked great. They were well fed, apparently not mistreated and they were given special treatment all around. They were allowed to go to Manila with Japanese escorts and they spent the nights in Bilibid Prison.

When they came back to Corregidor, they brought stories of cruel atrocities the Japanese inflicted on POWs there much like those we had experienced first-hand. They also carried rumors of Allied troops invading nearby islands and of the war coming to an end, which of course, proved to be just wishful thinking. It was still 1943, just a little more than a year after the fall of Corregidor. But none of us had any idea how much longer we would remain prisoners or how much time would pass before the war would finally end.

Scuttlebutt had run rampant about the disposition of the American greenbacks stored in the safe along with the silver coins at the military Headquarters in Malinta Tunnel. It was perhaps the last bright spot the guys on that particular detail would have for several years. They hauled the moneybags filled with bundles of greenbacks of different denominations out of the tunnel, emptied them into fifty gallon barrels, and set the green stuff on fire.

Sometimes a burning $20 bill would be used to light a cigarette, then the blackened remains would be nonchalantly dropped into the smoldering barrel. An expensive way to light a smoke, but this was the chance of a lifetime, to live the old adage "money to burn," particularly when there was no value in the money except to the Japanese and they would not have the opportunity to get their hands on it. One could only guess how much fun and how many good times were going up in flames. Of course, there were no places left to spend it and there was no one special to spend it on.

I mentioned earlier that after the fall of Corregidor all of us had become scavengers. Everything we found was picked up and fiercely protected regardless of the actual value. All of the stuff became precious to its owner and those who had special interests were usually able to find something that fulfilled their needs in one way or another.

There was a time when Big Band music circulated through the barracks area from an electric record player. A prized though small cache of seventy-eight records treated us to music and lyrics of the Big Band sound every evening after a long difficult day. This special music became a coveted connection to home and to our pre-war lives. One by one the records met their demise until there was only one left. It was a memorable recording of "I Don't Want to Set the World on Fire" by the Claude Thornhill orchestra.

I had enjoyed hearing it repeated many times night after night. One evening someone else obviously was no longer able to endure the repetition. At one point we all heard a loud, angry voice bellow, "Turn that damn thing off! I can't stand it anymore!" To our utter horror, we heard the screeching of the needle as it gouged across the surface of the record while being jerked off the turntable. Then came snapping sounds coupled with unrepeatable language as the record was crushed to bits in the hands of the disgruntled listener. Needless to say, that ended the "Big Band" era on Corregidor.

A notation across the top margin in the book of Genesis in Mother's Bible reads:

> June 8, 1943, boys from Topside were sent to Manila. First mass exodus we've experienced since the beginning of the year. Everyone expects us to do the like. June 11, Happy Birthday, Mother Dearest.

It was now June 30, 1943 and I was leaving Corregidor for the last time as a prisoner of war. I would not return again until 1967 as a civilian, once more in 1982, and for the last time in 1998. But those visits are another story.

As the throbbing engine powered the boat away from the pier, my mind reverted to April 1941 when I first laid eyes on the Rock—beautiful Corregidor Island. Despite the homesickness I had suffered, the difficulty of getting used to the heat, humidity, and the dreary rainy season, and not really liking the military life, as a whole, I discovered I quite enjoyed my nine months at Fort Mills on pre-war Corregidor. I found pleasure in the soft caress of the warm, tropical breeze on my face, the sedative sleep-inducing effect of the rain as it pelted the roof in the wee hours of the morning, the sweet nostalgia in the fragrance of the delicate white gardenia, the awe I felt at the vastness of the sea, the smell and the sounds of the waves lapping against the rocky cliffs. I was leaving it all behind, but I would always remember.

My life-long fascination with the sea began the summer I turned eighteen in 1936. A buddy of mine and I drove to Los Angeles hoping to find employment in one of the aircraft factories that was said to be paying wages far above those that we could earn in Salt Lake City. We didn't find work but I discovered the Pacific Ocean.

It was when I stood barefoot on the beach, pant legs rolled to my knees, gazing into the endless white-capped, blue-green waves while the water sucked the sand from beneath my feet, hearing the screams of the gulls above the roaring breakers, I decided I needed to spend some time near the sea. The boiling, churning froth of the surf had a mesmerizing effect on me. I was in love with one of Mother Nature's daughters.

Now I was leaving the sea and the grisly remains of the once lush green island behind, possibly forever. The destruction of Corregidor and her final demise had been a nightmare I had lived through. I would struggle for years to erase it from my mind. But I would always remember with deep feelings of satisfaction her sensuous tropical pleasures—the brilliant sunsets terminating abruptly into the sea and the resurrection of the sun in the morning from the depths of Manila Bay. I would never forget the sights and sounds of birds in the trees.

My whole being warmed as I recalled the special relationships formed with my fellow Americans as we worked those seemingly endless days and nights in the Malinta Tunnel Hospital. The bonds of friendship with those whose empathy and compassion had made my personal survival a reality would forever bind me emotionally to this place, so far removed from the safe security of my own country and my family. I would remember with great fondness Dr. Merkle, whose advice and warm friendship gave me a sense of belonging, confidence I could do my job while hoping for the termination of the nightmare we were living, and the patience he taught me through his example.

I would forever be indebted to General Moore for his compassion and understanding toward me when I had made a controversial but necessary decision, and when I became the victim of an honest mistake.

Smiling, I remembered the coveted romantic ideas concerning Lieutenant Young, the attractive young nurse who kept my mother's wedding ring from being confiscated by the Japanese. Had we met at a different time and place, perhaps our professional relationship could have developed into something more intimate and lasting. Perhaps.

I felt a deep sense of gratitude to Dr. McKissick, the short, heavy set dentist friend I worked with in the dental clinic of the Malinta Tunnel. He gave me hope and encouragement to look beyond prison camp, to work for my dental degree, then to set up practice with him in Odessa, Texas after the war. He helped me to believe in the future when life would once again be peaceful and stable.

Then there was the Japanese Major Horiuchi, who should have been my enemy, but who became my friend, whose kindness and respect for me as a human being helped me to heal physically as well as spiritually. I would never forget him. I smiled as I remembered "Major Horiuchi and his twelve 'Americans'", the displeasure and irritation we inflicted on the infamous old bastard, Major Lothrup!

I hoped I was also leaving behind the tortured memories of the ruthless treatment we had received at the hands of the enemy the first three months after the fall of Corregidor. The loathing repugnance the Japanese had expressed for us as Americans, as well as the bitterness and hatred that filled my heart for them would hopefully remain in the destruction and rubble of the once lovely, peaceful island.

The near hopeless acceptance of being a POW had been extremely difficult for me, but now I was feeling I could do what I needed to do for the moment and live one day at a time. Perhaps I would find hope for tomorrow as I ventured into new territory. Maybe I could endure to the end, whatever the end might be. Time would tell.

Before boarding the boat for Manila, we were subjected to one more inspection by the Japanese. These inspections were done whenever we were transferred from one place to another. We were required to lay everything we owned on the ground while a Japanese officer walked by and looked at our possessions, pitiful by usual standards, but nonetheless precious to us. Behind us would stand Japanese soldiers who watched to see that we didn't hide anything.

We learned very quickly when time came for an inspection nothing we had was truly ours. If there was anything the Japanese considered worth having, it was gone. We also became aware if we had any good clothing we should wear it, as we were allowed to keep anything that was on us. So the nearly worn out shirt was displayed on the ground with the other things and the not quite so worn one was on the back.

When I found out we were leaving for Manila, I went into the power house where on a shelf stood several ceramic jars containing mercury. I took one of them and put it into the empty rice bag holding my other meager possessions. The little jar was about six inches high, three inches in diameter and weighed about five pounds. The closure was tightly sealed with paraffin wax. Because of my experience in the Fort Mills and Tunnel dental clinics, I knew how essential the mercury was in making amalgam fillings, which are made by blending a silver alloy with mercury. The resulting amalgam is used for filling teeth in dentistry. It's initially silver in color, turning darker during the curing process. I knew it would be put to good use when I arrived at another prison camp if a dental clinic existed.

Some of the Japanese learned to speak English, or at least understand it. Out of necessity, all the prisoners learned enough Japanese to know our names and to understand and immediately obey orders given to us.

I was questioned several times about the contents of the heavy little ceramic jar before boarding the boat, again after we landed on Luzon, and yet again after my arrival at Bilibid Prison. My explanation seemed to satisfy all of the inquiries so no one tried to take it away from me. Neither the Japanese or other POWs seemed interested in it. It would prove to be more valuable than gold and very much appreciated by any of the dentists with whom I came in contact.

My reverie was interrupted when the boat bumped against the dock and I heard the order to go ashore. As I stepped onto the wharf of Luzon Island I wondered about Bilibid Prison. What awaited me there? I felt a bit apprehensive because I was indeed venturing into the unknown, but would very soon find out.

The approximate three mile march from the waterfront through Manila to Bilibid Prison was uncomfortable to say the least. It was hot with no rest periods and no water to drink. A notation in my mother's Bible dated June 30, 1943 said:

> Left Corregidor today for Bilibid Prison. Made it here without any trouble at all. Marched through Manila like we owned the place. Everyone was cheering and waving their arms.

I learned early that when the Japanese ordered us to march, usually in rows four abreast, that it was not a good thing to be on the outside of the line. To be so unlucky as to be number one or number four in the line was an open invitation to be kicked, slapped in the face, hit with a rifle butt or continually harassed by the Japanese escorts. I made it a practice to try and be number two or three in the line which afforded a bit more protection from all the abuse, but of course occasionally my luck ran out and I would get it again.

Bilibid prison, built during the Spanish occupation in the mid 1850, is located in the heart of downtown Manila surrounded by a high, wide masonry stone wall. It is designed in the shape of a wheel, the hub of the wheel being the central guard house where the guards could see all of the buildings around it that represented the spokes of the wheel. These brick buildings housed the prisoners and are long and narrow with high barred windows along the walls. The floors are concrete.

The Japanese were using Bilibid as a separation center and all of the prisoners were brought into this prison at one time or another. From here they were transferred to other prisons. Very often they would be shipped aboard the infamous "death ships" to Japan, Formosa, or Manchuria, where they would work as slave labor in the mines or steel mills. Bilibid was also the primary medical center for prisoners. Those who were very ill were brought in and kept in the hospital until well enough to work or until they died. A Bible entry on July 1st stated:

> Bilibid isn't so bad. The Navy has made quite the hospital out of it.

It was run by American Navy Pharmacy Chiefs. Among these friendly and efficient young men were several individuals I had known on Corregidor. I was so happy to see Chief Glen Slipsager, a good friend I met in the dental clinic in the Malinta Tunnel some time before the fall. Glen had come into the clinic one afternoon suffering excruciating pain from a throbbing toothache, hoping to find a dentist to extract the culprit. Since no one else was available, he asked if I could do it. Even though I had done several extractions, I was a bit nervous about it. I could see he was really hurting, so I consented. The tooth came out rather easily, to his relief and to mine.

We later spent some enjoyable time together chinning about our homes, family and friends. He had been raised in the midwest and we found we enjoyed a lot of the same things. In a short period of time we became good friends. Later, Glen was transferred to Bilibid Prison. I hoped to see him again, but I really didn't expect it to happen.

The pleasant reunion with Chief Slipsager was to be short lived—just a couple of weeks. That was the last time I saw Glen, or for that matter heard anything of him, until I became a dental student at the University of Missouri in Kansas City, Missouri in 1946. He had given me his sister Kathryn's address and telephone number in Lee's Summit, a suburb of Kansas City. I called her after my wife and I were settled in our apartment. She told us Glen had been declared missing in action and presumed dead as he had been aboard one of the unmarked infamous hell ships on its way to Japan when it was sunk by American torpedoes.

Another one of my friends who succumbed to the harsh realities of war was a Dr. Hearthneck who had been a dentist in the Malinta Tunnel. He received his excellent training in a Jesuit school in Chicago. He was transferred to Corregidor from Bataan with a group of nurses who were sent there pending the Japanese victory. I had gotten to know him very well as we worked together during the five months of fighting preceding the fall. An entry in Mother's Bible on July 10, 1943 recorded my sorrow when I learned of his death while he was a prisoner in Bilibid. He died days before I arrived. He was a fine man, an excellent dentist who taught me a great deal, and he was a dear friend. I wished I could have seen him once more.

Of course we were subjected to yet another inspection of our belongings when we reached Bilibid and were being checked in. The little ceramic jar containing the mercury was an item I had fiercely guarded and protected with explanations of its sole purpose and value. I would be glad to get it to the dental clinic in Cabanatuan and deliver it to the senior dental officer.

Even though my stay in Bilibid was to be short, nineteen days to be exact, because of my medical training and experience, I was assigned to a detail in the operating room in the hospital. When the doctors who were working there were not busy with wounded or the very ill, they were doing research on cadavers. They were trying to discover what effects dysentery, a debilitating and very often fatal disease, had on the body and why it was so deadly.

The obvious signs and symptoms were always the same, but there seemed to be more deep-seated reasons why some victims were able to fight it off and eventually regain their health awhile others succumbed to the ravages of this all too common disease. Perhaps the autopsies they were performing and the studies they did would reveal some secrets long hidden from the medical profession. The opportunity to use cadavers who died from its effects presented itself all too frequently. I was given the duty of cleaning up the surgery area after the exploratory research had been completed.

The cadavers' body fluids leaked in profusion onto the operating table, spilling onto the floor. As there were no rubber gloves available, I mopped up the area with my bare hands, using water with some sort of disinfectant to clean up the vile, smelly mess. With all of my previous training and experience as a medic I had never been subjected to that kind of nauseous duty. My hands would become raw from the harsh effects of the disinfectant and with the vigorous scrubbing when the repulsive task was completed. I would be glad to leave Bilibid, hopefully not to Japan!

Another good thing came from my interaction with the Navy Pharmacy Chiefs at the hospital. I was able to obtain a surgical scalpel which I used for a razor. When I first began the hospital detail I had complained about the fact I had not shaved since I left Corregidor. I don't remember what I traded for a much-used scalpel which was still quite sharp, and I was more than pleased. I hated growing a beard! A notation in my mother's Bible dated July 10, 1943 reads:

> Been signaling to some Filipino women today. Quite a thrill! It helps to pass the time away, but rather risky.

I guess men will be men, no matter what.

Sunday July 18, I wrote in Mother's Bible,

> Received word today that we are going to Cabanatuan, which incidentally is the largest prison camp in the Philippines.

Has had upwards of twenty-five hundred Americans die since the surrender.

The next morning we awakened early, hastily ate the usual issue of rice, and by dawn were ready to march to the railroad station. I felt uneasy but at the same time strangely eager for a change. I had not experienced a lot of negative interaction with the Japanese captors during the past few weeks at Bilibid, but I hadn't enjoyed the OR detail either.

After the three-mile march to the rail station, we were loaded onto metal box cars where we were packed together like sardines in a can. The ride was uncomfortably hot; perspiration flowed freely, breathing became difficult, and it seemed it would never end. According to the notation in Mother's Bible, dated July 19th:

Left Bilibid at 6:00 am for Cabanatuan, here at 2:00 pm after a ride in a box-car that was really awful to use for anything. Another march of a relatively few miles and we arrived at Prison Camp # 7. But now that I am here, it is not so bad.

8

CABANATUAN

After the cramped, oven-like conditions in those awful metal boxcars where we were vertically compressed and forced to stand up for several hours, it felt good to get my feet on the ground again and stretch my leg muscles. Even though the air was hot and heavy with humidity, it was a relief just to breathe freely again.

After we marched through the gate in the barbed wire fence which surrounded Cabanatuan, we were checked in at the Japanese Headquarters. Of course, the inevitable inspection was once again repeated. About the only thing of real value I had left was the little ceramic container of mercury. Once again, I explained its purpose. Then we stopped at the American Headquarters where we were assigned to our barracks.

We were to be housed with the Army internees in one of the long, bamboo, thatched roof barracks built on stilts. On each side of a dirt floor down the middle were sleeping bays built of split bamboo poles set a foot or so above the ground. Each prisoner was assigned one bunk area. The convex side of the poles where we were to lie down proved to leave a lot to be desired for minimal comfort. The concave sides were facing down where bed bugs and other insect communities resided.[41] I suppose most of us were too tired from our long, hot journey to care. All I wanted was something to eat and drink and time to lie down and rest.

---

41. Recollections of Wendell and other POW friends who remembered.

The lucky ones of the group had their own blankets which afforded warmth for the cool nights but gave little protection against the hordes of nocturnal bedbugs which came into our sleeping areas and feasted upon our naked bodies. Each morning when we awakened, the little bloody spots all over us bore mute evidence of their presence.

The next morning I delivered the ceramic container of mercury to the dental clinic. The primitive conditions under which the dentists were practicing shocked me. The equipment, most of it salvaged and battle scarred, was hardly adequate. Seeing the lack of medications and supplies, I knew the mercury would be a heaven-sent item.

I asked to see the senior dental officer, Colonel Albert Fields. When he saw the ceramic jar, he literally jerked it out of my hands. Without even a word of thanks, he turned and walked rapidly away to show his fellow dentists. He returned almost immediately with an apology for his behavior and ushered me inside his makeshift office where he thanked me profusely. Upon answering his questions as to where I had gotten the precious metal, as well as listening to the rehearsal of my recent personal history, he offered me a job as a technician in the dental clinic. He said he would take care of the details and I was to report for work the next morning after roll call, which I was more than happy to do. I was really glad for the dental experience I obtained when I worked in the Fort Mills hospital and in the Malinta Tunnel.

My job was to keep individual records of patient's work done as well as assist the dentist whenever I was needed. These records would be helpful to those concerned after the war. In addition they would be a means of identification in case of death. I hoped they were valuable, as paper of any kind to write on was scarce and very difficult to come by. As I remember, I used the back of milk can labels and some kinds of forms.

The work done here was mostly to relieve pain caused by multiple cavities and gum diseases, consequences of extended periods of time with little or no proper nutrition as well as lack of dental hygiene. As a result, most of the procedures were extractions which were usually done without the numbing effects of anesthesia of any kind. Occasionally minor surgery was performed under the same conditions.

I had been able to keep my teeth in better condition than some as I found a toothbrush in one of the pockets of my medic uniform. When I left the Malinta Tunnel I had Mother's Bible, a small bottle of vitamins, a container of silver nitrate crystals, and assorted first aid supplies in several pockets. I fiercely guarded them and miraculously had been able to keep some of them through the many inspections until the supply was exhausted. When the brush was no more, a swatch of fabric rubbed on a piece of hand soap sufficed for my morning and night tooth brushing ritual.

Names, some of them not entirely new to me, began to crop up in our conversations: malnutrition, wet and dry beri-beri, malaria, dengue fever, bacillary and amoebic dysentery, and protein anemia. Each name carried the dread of severe illness, and all too often, death. I had seen the effects of many of these diseases in the hospital at Bilibid so I was acquainted with them. But I had been very blessed or just plain lucky to have contracted none of them except for the bout of dengue fever I suffered before the fall of Corregidor.[42]

The Bilibid hospital was literally full of these disease cases. Many of the patients there were survivors of the Bataan Death March who were brought into the hospital nearly dead from these awful illnesses which were mostly caused by malnutrition or from the dreaded mosquito bites.

In spite of continued exposure to conditions which may have warranted my becoming ill, as well as the nutritional deficiencies, I remained healthy. My medical training as well as the basic rules of good hygiene taught me by my mother to "wash my hands often and never, never eat anything I picked up from the ground" also contributed to that fact.

By the time I left Corregidor for the last time, the "buddy system" was in full swing. If you didn't have a buddy, someone you could trust to take care of you when you were ill and couldn't do things for yourself when you got well enough to go back to your

---

42. McGarry talk, Manti High School, 1993.

daily routine or when you came back from a detail, you would often come back to nothing. All of your things were gone—clothes, shoes, and anything else you thought was necessary to sustain life were no more. There was definitely a dog-eat-dog atmosphere, but the buddy system helped somewhat to alleviate the problem.[43]

My first buddy was a guy who had lost an arm. Everyone referred to him as the "one armed bandit." He was a good guy and I am not sure what happened to him as we were separated when I left Corregidor to go to Fort Frank.

Shortly after getting settled into the routine at Cabanatuan, I became acquainted with several of the guys in the dental clinic. Two of the medical personnel I enjoyed visiting with and getting to know well were Sam Palasota and Gus Davis. We worked together, then we became "mess buddies." While we ate we reminisced about our homes, our parents and our growing up years. We became friends, sharing our post-war dreams and confidences. I looked forward to our "dining" talks. Those were good times to remember in a setting where there was not much good of any kind to be found. They were transferred to Bilibid where we met again and were finally liberated together in February 1945.

There were three other young men who were in my squad with whom I formed a very close relationship when we became "quan" members. "Quan" is a word borrowed from Tagalog one of the many dialects spoken in the Philippine Islands where it is spelled *kuwan*. This word was used in the prison camps and means to cook together or in reference to food. As time went on other meanings were attached to "quan." It became commonplace in the American jargon used in prison camp.[44]

As 1943 lengthened into autumn, food became more scarce and the workloads increased. It was about this time that the Japanese allowed the prisoners to cultivate small areas of ground and grow a limited variety of vegetables to supplement the daily ration of mushy rice lugao.

---

43. Ibid.
44. Ibid

Everett Turney from Modesto, California, Ed Underwood from Knoxville, Tennessee, Earnest Crunkleton from Everton, Kansas, and I became a quan. We pooled our resources of crude cooking utensils and did our own cooking of the vegetables we were allowed to grow. I remember the okra and eggplant we cooked and ate together. For some reason I have not been able to see, smell, or eat either of those vegetables ever again. However, rice is a staple food in our home, but the butter, salt, and sometimes sugar are vital to the taste and enjoyment of it.

Crunkleton had possession of a little hand-held device that ground rice into a fine flour. Using his entrepreneurial inclinations, he found plenty of customers for whom he would grind three cups of rice flour in return for one cup of the finished product. We used the flour to supplement our food menu with a flat bread and whatever else we could find.

The four of us became protectors of each other and our meager possessions. When there was illness or we had to go on details away from camp, we policed our little garden and we watched very carefully that no one was allowed to steal anything belonging to us. The dog-eat-dog atmosphere of the camp was fostered mostly by hunger when prisoners turned into predatory animals stealing with an air of utter disregard for anyone but themselves. Trusted friends became priceless.

It was in 1943, close to a year after the surrender, when the Army Command came into being. A semblance of order was born with American officers in charge of various groups of military units. Authority brought with it mostly effective leadership, which was badly needed, and some observance of rules and regulations. This mode of governing the prison camp society was slow to mature and presented many challenges but it almost became of age with use and with the passage of time. Then punishment came for the gangs of bullies who had roamed through the prison camps right after the fall, taking what they wanted. Order was restored. Of course, all of this, though far from perfect, was done under the direct scrutiny and approval of the Japanese Command. "The enemy then became our sole adversary, waiting, wondering, trying to stay alive, our burden."[45]

---

45. Ibid.

As in all areas of society, there are those who will take advantage of others if given the slightest opportunity. This happened frequently with some of the American officers in Cabanataun. Many were arrogant, rude, and extremely obnoxious. They placed themselves on pedestals, demanding special consideration in food, lodging, and in the work required by the Japanese. And when the Japanese decided to compensate the prisoners for their work, the officers received from eighty pesos to two hundred twenty pesos a month, depending on their rank. A buck private earned fifteen pesos a month for his labor.

Of course, there were those officers who were excellent administrators before the war; fair, honest and considerate of the men in their charge. They remained steadfast but seemed to be in the minority. I was fortunate to have rubbed shoulders with many of the really good ones with whom I worked in the medical field, and just a few of the other kind.

In addition to General Moore, my Commanding Officer on Corregidor, three of the special officers I formed close relationships with were Major Emil Merkle, MD, Major J.T. McKissick, DDS, and Colonel Albert Fields. DDS.

Dr. Merkle and I were good friends on Corregidor. I had been fortunate to have formed an even closer relationship with him during the nine months I stayed on Fort Frank. I was overjoyed to meet him again in the hospital at Cabanatuan where we were able to spend a fair amount of time together, further cementing our friendship.

Major McKissick was a dentist who worked in the Dental Clinic in the Malinta Tunnel. I met him again in Cabanatuan and, amazingly enough, again in Bilibid Prison where I was sent a second time in October 1944. We came home together after the liberation.

Colonel Fields was very good to me after I delivered the mercury to him. We became close friends as we worked. I lost track of him after my transfer to Bilibid until I began dental training in Kansas City. One day I saw him going up a staircase in one of the buildings at the University and I could scarcely believe my eyes. He was teaching diagnostics, one of the classes I was to attend. It was very pleasant to renew our friendship in a much more positive environment. We exchanged Christmas greetings every year until he died in 1987.

I was totally excited one day while I was on duty in the hospital at Cabanatuan when I met another one of the survivors of the Bataan Death March. After a brief conversation, I discovered he was from my home town, Salt Lake City. Although this was our first meeting, it was wonderful to find someone from home. Robert Strasters, a surgery technician, and I immediately formed a friendship that was to bond us together through many difficult times in our post-war years. When I left Cabanatuan, Bob was still there. He was one of the five hundred remaining prisoners who were liberated by the daring rescue efforts of the 6th Ranger Battalion in January of 1945.[46]

Shortly after I arrived at Cabanatuan, the prisoners were all placed in groups of ten men. This was done as a deterrent to escape attempts that were continually occurring among the desperate prisoners. The rule stated that if one of the group escaped, the other nine were to be shot. For this reason they were called "shooting squads." The element of trust seemed to be weak and almost missing at times, and rightly so, among the squad as escape attempts were continually being made. So each of us closely watched the other nine on a regular basis for any signs of escape preparations—or even thoughts of it.

Although I was not personally aware of any instances where the remaining nine were shot, I heard from other prisoners who had witnessed these mass murders that it had, in fact, happened. I did see some very harsh treatment being meted out to the perpetrators as well as the other squad members if an escape was attempted. No one in my squad made any such foolish attempts. However, I witnessed a disturbing event which resulted in one of many murders by the Japanese guards. On October 23rd, I wrote briefly in my mother's Bible:

> Dearest Mother, today they took an American out to measure him for his grave! Poor boy escaped from camp and was caught.

---

46. When Wendell and Bob Strasters renewed their friendship in Salt Lake City, Bob told McGarry of his amazing liberation from Cabanatuan by the 6th Army Rangers in January 1945.

In September of 1943 rumors were wildly circulating throughout Cabanatuan. Prisoners coming into the camp brought all kinds of wonderful news, mostly concerning the US winning the war which would mean, of course, our freedom. I had heard there was a radio hidden somewhere within the barbed wire enclosure that was home to so many young Americans. I never did see it nor did I have any concrete knowledge as to the exact whereabouts, but I looked forward to hearing the radio reports that verified some of the rumors about how the war was going. I wrote in Mother's Bible on September 9th:

> Italy has fallen, news sounds like something, here's hoping.

It seemed that hope was all we had to hang on to.

At one time we were told the date that we were to be released, which proved to be fictitious, but which once again lifted our spirits for a while. I wrote in mom's Bible dated September 17, 1943:

> I am hanging on for September 30th, the date of our release
> I believe.

But the waiting game for release soon came to an abrupt end and we reentered into the doldrums of prison life once again.

I had taken up smoking when I was in my late teens. My dad had an unwritten rule about smoking after eating. "When you light up a cigarette, you're finished with your meal, no more food, dessert, anything. You are full." I used this as a mental assurance that when I took a puff or two of a cigarette butt, I did it because my stomach was full. I really did not need any more to eat. It never completely took away the hunger, but it eased the pangs to a point where I could function and push the thoughts of food, at least somewhat, into the back of my mind.

It worked until the evening hours before bedtime when the prisoners sat around in groups and talked of food: Thanksgiving, Christmas, special birthday meals, ordinary everyday breakfasts, lunch or dinner menus, wonderful meals that our mothers or wives prepared. Recipes for real or imagined delicacies were exchanged. It was crazy but it served to give those involved a weird kind of high that nothing else seemed to accomplish.

Something even more interesting to me was hearing the guys discuss where they lived and how they were raised. I made mental notes and came to the conclusion that the boys raised on farms or in small towns had better childhoods than those of us who were raised in the cities. The rural residents had more freedom, probably because of safety issues, than city kids did. These guys spoke fondly of their childhood friends, neighbors, ball games, picnics, and riding horses through the pastures.

They were able to hike into the hills, walk to the corner drug store and to the movies. They spent a lot more time out of doors doing chores and playing physical games than I did as a child.

I decided then and there when I got home, received my dental degree, and was ready to go into practice, I would definitely prefer to live in and raise my future family in a small town. I hoped the girl I left behind was still waiting and would become a part of that equation. The thought was good and it gave me a mental goal to look forward to, dream about, and plan for when I was a free man again.

We indulged in this kind of conversation night after night until all of us knew everything there was to know about everyone else. We even became bored with the tales that "Pete the Pimp," a kid from New York City told us about helping his father manage a stable of prostitutes. Of course he would go into minute, graphic details of the sordid business, but it wasn't long until the conversation would drift back to food, the preparation, and the eventual indulgence thereof.

Then there was this pathological liar who, no matter what subject was broached, knew all there was to know about it. In fact he was even able to narrate in precise detail how to perform several surgical procedures. After one such report, I asked Dr. Merkle if he thought the guy had actually performed such an operation. My surgeon friend replied, "It beats the hell out of me."

Late in 1943, the Japanese lifted the restrictions on POWs receiving packages. Many of these boxes had been assembled and readied for shipment by Red Cross volunteers. They could then be purchased by families to send to their loved ones overseas.

After I arrived home I read a report written by Mrs. George Garrett in the *Prisoners of War Bulletin, Volume 2, No.1, January*

1944. It was published by the American Red Cross for relatives of American, international POWs and civilian internees. It indicated these centers were open five days a week. Apparently there were four Prisoners of War Food Packaging centers in the U.S., located at Philadelphia, Chicago, New York, and St. Louis, which were operated by women in their spare time. They ran two shifts every day with eighty workers on each shift. The report also stated that during 1943 these women volunteers produced over seven million standard food packages for American and Allied prisoners of war. Mrs. Garrett further related an extraordinary example of the demands on these workers.

> An emergency call for 180,000 parcels to be delivered to the ship *Gripsholm* in four and one half days was given in the last week of August, 1943. As many of the regular volunteers were on vacations, older men, women, and young boys and girls stepped in to fill the worker gap. The order was filled in less than the allotted time, delivered to the waiting ship, and the packages were thought to be in the hands of most of the prisoners in the Far East by Christmas.[47]

When I returned home after the liberation, I was amazed to learn how the women of the United States had stepped up to the plate during the war. They had gone all out to help win the victory along with their fighting men. Most of these women, both single and married, had full time jobs in sewing plants making uniforms, in small arms plants manufacturing guns and ammunition, in ship yards welding ships and submarines, in airplane factories turning out fighters and bombers by the thousands, in former automobile plants manufacturing GI Jeeps and welding tanks together. These women were the home front army who supplied the troops with the necessities of war.

"Rosie the Riveter" posters were plastered all over billboards, buildings, inside buses, and in crowded airports and train stations. They featured the image of a woman in work clothes, hair tied up in a bandanna in an attitude of power and strength

---

47. Garrett, Mrs. George. *Prisoner of War Bulletin*, Vol. 2, Number 1, 1944, Washington, D.C., 3. Mail for POW in the Far East.

emphasized by a look of absolute determination on her face. She became the female icon of the home front war effort. In addition to becoming the factory assembly line worker, Rosie represented all the women who stepped into the role of Dad as well as Mom while raising families. And she kept the traditional home fires burning in anticipation of the return of sweethearts, husbands, and fathers.[48]

Up to this time, few married or single women had found employment in any work areas except teachers, secretaries, waitresses, nurses, domestic help or clerks in stores. But as the war progressed and most of the young men were pressed into military service, the young women went to work outside their homes into jobs formerly held by men. Grandparents and other relatives tended the children.[49]

On weekends, preteens and teenagers alike went house to house collecting cardboard, newspapers, clean mashed tin cans with the lids tucked inside, and great rolls of tinfoil for recycling. Everyone made their own contribution to the war effort. Everything was geared to "after the war," or "when the war is over."[50]

As former prisoners, we remember rumors of the arrival of the Red Cross packages circulating through Cabanatuan early in November, 1943 but most of them were not delivered to the prisoners until the Japanese had inspected them and in some cases had taken what they wanted from the boxes. On December 1st the notation across the top of a page in the little Bible stated:

> Red Cross packages came into camp. Nothing makes me more homesick. If you could only understand how good old American food makes you feel, you could cry with joy to realize that you no longer have to save for the day that provisions might run out and you would starve. Yes, if you could only know.

We all waited anxiously for our names to be called to receive a coveted box. I carried my precious package to my quarters

---

48. Rosie the Riveter, Wikipedia < http://en.wikipedia.org/wiki/Rosie_the_Riveter>.
49. Friends and family told me of these things when I returned to Salt Lake City in 1945.
50. McGarry, Gwen, memories as a teenager during the war.

and opened it. Then I sat down and stared at the treasurers for several moments before I touched any of them. This box had a polo shirt, soap, shaving cream and brush, razor blades, comb and case, socks, towel, tooth brush, tooth powder, pencils, checkers and chess board, playing cards, prunes, raisins, wash cloth, vitamin tablets, safety pins, cheese, a small mirror, cigarettes, and Ovaltine. I found a list of these things on a customs declaration post card among my pre-war letters my Mother had saved. The total value was listed as $4.66. It was postmarked August 30, 1943, from New York City. Sender was listed as the American Red Cross. Many of the items I later traded for things I wanted, mostly food.

This was the first thing I had received from home in almost two years. No letters, nothing to give me a connection with the United States, nothing to assure me I still had a home and a family. The pain of separation from those I loved, the nostalgia, mixed with a consuming sense of gratitude filled my heart and I shed tears of pure joy. December 8th, the following Bible notation says:

> Still nothing has happened here and almost two years have passed since I received word from home. Rumors at camp say that letters from home will soon be here. I hope to God it's true and everything is OK. I don't believe I'm quite calloused enough to take a family setback now even though I won't worry about it. Secretly I have been hoping that Mary Louise Merrill would write me, too, although she takes an inferior seat compared to you and to your health, Mother darling. I still weigh one hundred thirty pounds but I am losing my hair. Too bad. Still it is alright.

It was not until I returned to Salt Lake City after the war I discovered my parents had received word, a postcard from me, not the war department, stating I was alive and a POW in August, 1943. Up to that time I had been declared "Missing in Action" after the fall of Corregidor. It was several months after receiving this word that the Japanese allowed letters to be delivered to us.

A printed directive stated the conditions for letters written to the POWs:

1. Letters must be less than 25 words in length.
2. Letters must be typewritten or legibly block printed.
3. Subject matter must be strictly personal; no military or political matters or opinions may be included.
4. The name of the Internment Camp must appear in the forwarding address.

These conditions have been imposed by the Japanese Government and not by the U.S. Government.[51]

Communications allowed to be sent to families by POWs were postcards with a form letter on them filled out by the internee:

1. I am interned at–Philippine Military Prison Camp No.____.
2. My health is–excellent; good; fair; poor.
3. Message _____Signature.[52]

After my parents received the first communication from me sometime in late August, 1943, a press release from the *United Press* in Washington D.C. dated September 2nd, along with my picture, was published in the *Salt Lake Tribune*. It stated my parents had received a card from me confirming that I was a POW of the Japanese in the Philippine Islands. I did not receive any communication from Mom and Dad until after Christmas in Cabanatuan.

After my parents learned of the fall of Corregidor my mother wrote a letter with several pages. It was returned to her and a little printed sign on the back of the envelope said:

RETURN TO SENDER
BY SENSOR
SERVICE SUSPENDED

She wrote to the war department asking for instructions as to communicating with me and she received the aforementioned directive.

My heart ached for my parents after the fall of the Philippines, and I had been extremely concerned for the mental anguish I knew they were suffering in not knowing of my fate. But I felt the influence of the prayers they were saying in my behalf. My

---

51. Directive from War Department concerning letters to POWs.
52. Directive from War Department concerning letters from POWs.

sister later told me one day she had opened Mother's bedroom door and found her on her knees at her bedside tearfully begging the Lord to let her know where her son was and how he was. She never quit believing I was alive.

After receiving that first letter from my parents, I shed tears of relief and gratitude in finding that those I loved were alive and well. The sensation of hope filled my heart and through my tears I silently thanked my Heavenly Father.

It was nearly Thanksgiving 1943. I began dreaming about my family being together in that little home where I was raised in Salt Lake City. I could virtually see the long table covered with a snow-white cloth set with Mother's good dishes and flatware. I could almost smell the turkey and dressing baking in the oven. My mouth watered when I remembered the taste of the hot rolls dripping with butter, smothered in Mother's homemade jam, and the fluffy mashed potatoes and gravy. The thought of the pumpkin pie heaped with whipping cream was pure torture.

My parents and my older siblings would be there with their families, the exception being the brother just older than I who may have joined the ranks of the military. My two younger brothers as well as my two brothers-in-law were probably away somewhere fighting in Europe. The rumors circulating around camp indicated the fighting there was hot and heavy. I prayed for my siblings who were involved in wartime activities. I earnestly begged my Heavenly Father for their protection and for the well being of my mother and dad.

Occasionally I had been rotated out of the dental clinic to do other details. I was glad to avoid some of them, but it was good to do the wood cutting detail. Although it was hard work, I enjoyed going outside the confines of the wire enclosure of Cabanataun. Thanksgiving Day happened to be one of these times. I left on the detail early in the morning with a promise from Ed Underwood, one of my quan buddies, that he would save me some of the Thanksgiving feast.

A dog had been caught in one of the traps the enterprising POWs had set and it was to be our Thanksgiving dinner. Everyone looked forward to the prospect of actually having meat to eat, even if it was something that we would never have considered as food for human beings in a free society. As I remember, the dog was skinned, gutted, then filled with a mixture of rice and any herbs and spices that could be scrounged up. It was then cooked over an open fire until time for dinner.

When I returned to camp, it was quite dark, and after a hard day's labor I was eager to have a good meal, but Ed informed me the meat was gone and all that remained of the Thanksgiving dinner I had thought about all day was the wretched rice. I was disappointed, but hungry enough to devour it as if it were what I expected.

Every Thanksgiving Day after we returned home I called Ed or he called me. The conversation always began in the same manner. If it were me calling him, I would say: "Is this the SOB who ate all the dog for Thanksgiving?" Or he would immediately say after I answered the telephone, "This is the SOB who ate all the dog for Thanksgiving!" Then we would laugh before having our usual catch-up-on-our-lives conversation. After Ed passed away, I missed that call on the Thanksgiving holiday but I never failed to think about him and the dog that I'm now glad I didn't get to eat.

I continually thought of my family the duration of my imprisonment. I wished desperately that I could see and talk to them, but I had pretty much accepted the impossibility of my fate as fact. However, it was during the coming of the holiday season I once again experienced the sharp pangs of homesickness and longing for days that used to be.

When I closed my eyes I envisioned the freshly cut evergreen tree standing in front of Mother's living room window decorated with little colored lights, shiny glass balls and strings of popped corn. I ached to hear the Christmas carols floating through the frosty winter air mixed with the chatter of excited children anticipating the arrival of St. Nick.

I missed the snow falling to earth in great, fluffy flakes transforming our neighborhood into a fairyland of white that sparkled and shimmered in the light of a full moon. I missed my family. I missed my sweetheart! I needed to feel the love that comes with the indisputable sense of belonging. Dreaming of home at holiday time became bittersweet. My heart was filled with intense longing. I prayed for comfort, for peace, for deliverance.

It was some time after the arrival and distribution of the Red Cross packages an officer I did not know came to me and asked if I knew Major Merkle. I said I did. He told me Dr. Merkle was being transferred to Japan. A group of officers who had access to extra food would like to give him a going-away party. Did I want to help?

Certainly I was anxious to help give my dear friend a proper send off, even though I was filled with sadness to have him go. I was fairly sure if he went to Japan I would never see him again. In answer to my query as to what I could do, the officer told me if I would give him several cigarettes he would make arrangements for the food. That sounded like a deal!

A trio of musicians who for some time had played their versions of the Big Band music for the prisoners as well as the Japanese agreed to do the entertainment. I gave each of them a cigarette for their services. That was all I had to do. In essence my contribution of tobacco would pay for the whole party. I handed over the precious, probably quite stale, Lucky Strike or Camel cigarettes, and a great time was had by all!

It was in 1990 my second wife and I attended the Northwest Chapter of the American Defenders of Bataan and Corregidor Reunion in Sand Point, Idaho. In route we stopped in Hayden, Idaho and visited with Dr. Merkle and his wife Juanita. Forty-seven years after the incident had taken place it was then he asked me if I knew anything about his going away party at Cabanatuan in 1943. All through the years he had been very curious about who was responsible for it as the officers who invited him to come as an honored guest were complete strangers to him. I told him I had paid for the party with cigarettes but I, too, had no idea who the officers were or how they knew I had been hoarding the tobacco to do some serious trading. I just assumed they were his friends. We never did solve the puzzle but it provided some speculative conversation and some good laughs.

Tobacco was the preferred item of choice for barter. It would pay for anything available. If one of the prisoners had something a person with cigarettes wanted, a deal could be struck to the satisfaction of both parties. There were guards who would also make scarce items, usually food they had smuggled into camp, available in exchange for cigarettes. They loved the American tobacco because it was more mild and better tasting than the Japanese variety.

I traded cigarettes for a much-appreciated service from a fellow prisoner who had a small monkey he kept on a chain. This little fellow loved to eat bugs. I suppose the bedbugs infesting our bedding was a delicacy. He was more than willing to forage the pesky insects out of the bedding and mosquito netting. He was even able to remove the head lice in our hair and we were more than willing to pay his master for the services.

It was in December of 1943 when a Japanese officer passing through Cabanataun asked to see me. He was one of Major Horiuchi's men on Corregidor and he brought me a carton of Japanese cigarettes. They were extremely strong and smelly, which didn't seem to matter as I was able to trade them for food. I was grateful for a new resource which I'm sure helped to sustain my life and those in my quan, even though we all continued to lose weight. By the time I was liberated early in 1945 my normal weight of one hundred fifty-five pounds had dropped to less than one hundred pounds.

When the supply of American cigarettes became extinct, dried tobacco leaves were available at the commissary. They were purchased, crushed and rolled into harsh-tasting, tongue-biting, cigarettes which gave off clouds of foul-smelling smoke. Pages from the GI Bibles that some of us still had provided the paper to "roll your own." If you were lucky enough to have read the scripture before using it in this manner, the guilt trip didn't seem quite so severe. If not, it just didn't matter. Though crudely constructed, these cigarettes seemed to satisfy the nicotine addicts.

I am not sure just when the commissary came into being, but it was doing business by the time I arrived at Cabanatuan. I understood some of the POWs had money when they came and were able to pool their resources. With the blessing of the Japanese Command, the commissary was established. There was a limited supply of foodstuffs, cigarettes, and fresh fruits which appeared intermittently, how and exactly from what source I didn't know. But it was good to supplement our diets of grossly overcooked, salt-less rice lugao.

When bananas came in, the large, fat ones were saved for the officers. What was left was sold to the enlisted men, at the same price, I might add. It did no good to resent this type of situation or try to remedy it. Most of us just learned to accept it and let it go. It was just another way the unfair political system worked in prison camp. But I think we all remembered.

It has become second nature to me to always buy the large, fat, yellow, "officers bananas" whenever I go into the super market. Subconsciously I suppose I never want to feel that kind of discrimination ever again.

It was early into 1944 that food became more of a premium. The rice rations decreased in quantity, there were only two meals a day, and the items we previously were able to purchase in the commissary went completely away.

There was a large camp farm outside the prison's wire fence where rice and a variety of fresh vegetables were grown. It had been planted, weeded, irrigated, and harvested by POWS, but very little of it found its way into the camp kitchens or into the canteen cup to assist in sustaining our lives.

At one time or another everyone would have a detail to work on the farm. Sometimes it was possible to sneak and eat a dirty vegetable but it was risky business. If you were caught it was more than probable you would receive another beating. In fact, the certainty was so great some of us, no matter how hungry we were, would not take the chance. Those who did and were caught paid a heavy penalty, sometimes with life itself.

In certain situations the passage of time has a way of melding one day into another until time itself has little or no meaning. The days in prison camp became a blur of doing basically the same things, the consuming boredom, smelling the stench of the dead, the uncertainty and fear of who would be next. First and foremost was the ever-present hunger the tasteless portions of rice or stewed bitter pig weed failed to appease. "The demand for work went on, rations got smaller, the dying continued to die."[53]

---

53. McGarry talk, Manti High School, 1993.

Was it the lack of nutrition I needed to sustain my immune system, the increased work details I had been on, or my continued weight loss causing me to suffer through several recent bouts of malaria? Even though swarms of mosquitoes were everywhere, I had avoided becoming ill for a long while. But work in the hospital had become more stressful. There were more gravely ill patients to care for, and more dying. My strength was wearing down.

May 11, 1944 this rumor was recorded in Mother's Bible:

> Have heard that the Japanese do not want these Americans to be retaken—so now I don't know what to expect. In fact I don't really know how to take it whether or not they shoot us is just another thing to think about. Pleasant thought!

The two-year anniversary of our imprisonment came with May, 1944. The year slowly passed into summer, autumn and into the tropical winter. I sensed a change had come over me. I felt a deterioration of my mind, my attitude, as well as my body was occurring. I came to the realization this very thing was happening in all the prisoners around me. Every one of us had given up all hope of imminent liberation.

Our bodies became weakened, exhausted, prematurely old, our minds dull and unresponsive. I found I had become almost past feeling. My senses were numbed to a point where my hatred for the Japanese, my impossible predicament, the nostalgia and longing for home, seemed to be almost the norm. I felt neither joy nor sadness, comfort or pain. I was teetering precariously on the edge of just not caring anymore.

The only thing I was fully aware of was the ever present, gnawing hunger that nagged, annoyed, and continually persisted. I eventually came to the realization I might not survive one more beating, one more day of starvation, one more day of not knowing. My mind had evolved into a state of nothingness, dragging my exhausted body with it.

Desperation leads individuals into strange and sometimes weird paths of behavior. I was feeling so extremely lonely and devoid of hope that in my mind, I searched for something I could cling to, something I could do that was mine alone, something very private, secret from the enemy, something they could not take away from me. I began to whistle. It was not a shrill or even a musical sound. Actually it could hardly have been called a real whistle. Rather it was just a slightly audible "whew, whew, whew" as I exhaled breath between my front teeth and barely pursed lips. Strangely enough this gave me a feeling of strength, security, and safety in my own little realm. Time became of little consequence. When I indulged in this idiosyncrasy I harbored a feeling of personal defeat of the enemy.

I could be myself and do what I wanted without fear of reprisal of any kind from them. This was my privacy and I did it because I could. This strange little habit became a part of me that I took home and practiced frequently throughout the rest of my life without explanation or apology.

In spite of the lack of positive emotions I mustered up what remained of my ebbing strength and earnestly prayed for an answer to a question I had posed to my Heavenly Father on numerous occasions. I needed to know. Was I going to endure to the end of this dreadful experience? Was I going to live through it or was I going to die?

Throughout the time I had been a prisoner, the past few months in particular, I witnessed dozens of deaths that occurred when the victims just gave up. They would lie down and die virtually for the lack of any incentive to fight, to hang on, to live. I still had just enough life left in me I needed to know. It was in this frame of mind I had gone to bed after petitioning the Lord for an answer to my plea. Even after these many years I am not exactly sure what happened that eventful evening. The answer came quietly, clearly, and beyond a shadow of a doubt. I found myself within a vision or a dream.

I was walking slowly down a long corridor which appeared to be a hospital. In the distance I saw a group of men, women and children. They were milling around a hospital bed wherein lay an elderly man. The sparse white hair accentuated the pale face, the voice was weak, and the speech halting. The attitude was one of farewell to his wife and family. He was dying.

As I neared the group I was stunned by what I saw. A surprised gasp escaped my lips as I recognized the elderly man.

The old guy who was on his death bed saying good-bye to his loved ones was me! It was then I knew, as a quiet voice within me whispered very clearly, "Yes, you are going to make it. You will live to fulfill your destiny."

I knew I was not going to die in this miserable prison camp. I was going to live! I was going to have a wife and the opportunity to raise a family of my own. I was going to make it home. Tears of unfathomable gratitude coursed down my cheeks, the sweetness of hope welled up in my breast and I humbly thanked my Heavenly Father.

While I was still in this state of amazed joy, my fingers slid along the belt of my ragged trousers until I could feel my mother's wedding band securely pinned inside. Excitement mounted within me as I whispered, "Yes, Mother darling, I'm going to bring it back to you, just like I promised. I am coming home."

I don't remember a great deal more about events that transpired at Cabanatuan after that experience, but I do know new life had been transfused into my body by the assurance I was given concerning my future.

The will to live, to survive whatever time remained of my Prisoner of War experience, had been renewed and I knew I could do what I needed to do. I had no idea how much longer this hell would continue, but I did know I would face it, I would fight back and I would win!

9

BACK TO BILIBID

I was shipped from Cabanatuan back to Bilibid and arrived there to begin work at the hospital on October 21, 1944. According to a list of those who were taken back at the same time, the names of two of my quan buddies, Everett Turney and Ed Underwood, appeared on the list as well. Crunkleton's name was not on it.[54] I don't know what happened to him as we had no further contact after the war ended.

I hoped to see some of my Navy pharmacy chief friends at Bilibid. They had done such a good job of running the hospital when I was there in 1943. The hospital had since been taken over by the Army with Major Warren Wilson as the Chief Medical Officer. He was an eye, ear, nose and throat M.D. from Los Angeles. He became my friend and our relationship would continue after the war. He was Colonel Wilson when he died in 1984.

Rumors continued to run rampant during September and October of 1944 before I left Cabanatuan. We continued to hear more and more of the defeat of the Imperial Japanese forces. Notations in mother's Bible stated that U.S. forces had taken Wake, Guam, Okinawa, most of New Britain and New Guinea, which appeared to be true. Then in September 1944 we heard Germany had fallen. Noted in Mother's Bible, September 16th:

---

54. A list of all the POWs who served under the command of Major Wilson at Bilibid between October 21, 1944 and February 5, 1945 was given to Wendell by Walter Pankratz a medic with whom he had worked in the Malinta Tunnel Hospital on Corregidor before the fall. Walter was also liberated at Bilibid and came home on the *AE Anderson*.

News of news! Heard that Germany has surrendered, boy oh boy, do you know what that means, Mother, darling? And the best of all is that I can receive word from you-you who hold everything in the world for me. To think of what I want to do for you, to try and make up for the suffering that you've endured. Oh Mother—I can't explain it, but you're my world—to think—to be able to go anywhere with you, anywhere, no guards, no Japanese influence. It's what will make life worth living once more.

Then September 17th:

News flew through the camp like wildfire, about Germany yesterday, now today no one will confirm it. All possible resources have been closed up. Oh, please, God! Let it be so about Germany.

September 30th:

Well, dearest Mother the news up to now doesn't seem to be any good at all. Who, who knows how long I'll be here-I don't! The food around here is getting slim too. So again there you are-rice, and tea with mushy rice for breakfast. Boy, food like this really makes you think of home! The U.S. is winning the war and will soon launch an invasion.

But then, we had heard all of this before only to be let down with no more evidence to substantiate rumor into fact. (Germany did not actually surrender until May 7, 1945.)

When we first heard the unmistakable drone of an airplane engine coming in our direction, we were certain that it was Japanese. Then we actually witnessed an American P38 aircraft shoot down a Japanese Zero outside Cabanatuan. We were totally delighted. We became believers.

This amazing incident and subsequent events made the Japanese guards jumpy. They became nervous, short tempered, irritable, and it was impossible to predict their reactions in any situation. They were obviously afraid of what the immediate future would hold for them. To their complete discomfort, U.S. aircraft flew over the camp frequently.

At first we ran out into the open spaces cheering and waving at the low flying aircraft. Then the Japanese ordered us to remain indoors whenever a plane flew over. These most welcome signs of U.S. victory served to give us hope, but at the same time accelerated our impatience for our final release. The stress and strain of work under the continued harassment of the beleaguered guards coupled with the constant hunger contributed to making this another very unpleasant time in prison camp.

I was glad to be back at Bilibid. At least for the present I would be sleeping in a real brick building in a real bunk. I never did become completely comfortable on the thin lumpy mattress which I expected to be a step up in comfort from the split bamboo poles I had slept on for many months.

When my wife and I visited Bilibid Prison in 1998 it was still being used by the city of Manila. The same red brick building where I bunked was still there, filled with high bunk beds and inhabited by women prisoners, one of whom had just delivered a tiny baby girl.

I found when I began work in the hospital I did, indeed, have several friends still there. A couple of the Navy pharmacists, close associates of Glen Slipseager, and Dr. McKissick, my dentist friend from Texas, were in the dental clinic. Seeing old friends helped me to make another adjustment to shorter rations and continual details. "When I discovered food rations were even tighter here than had been at Cabanatuan, I was at a body weight that less food and the demand for more work would barely support."[55]

Most of the prisoners already in Bilibid were hospitalized, desperately ill, and in need of more care and medications than we could possibly supply. But the knowledge I would eventually return home sustained me to do the best I could.

I worked mostly in the hospital or the dental clinic but I was assigned to do an occasional detail outside the prison walls as well. I awoke early on such a morning with a raging fever. Even though I had been designated as one of the "working well," I was really sick, probably with dengue fever, but I climbed on to the truck that was to take us to wherever. I do not remember

---

55. McGarry talk, Memorial Day, Ephraim, Utah, 1997.

anything about that detail, where I was, or what I had been doing. I somehow survived the struggle of the day and when we returned that evening, Dr. McKissick met me, helped me off the truck, administered seconol, a sedative, and put me to bed.

My bunk was near the top. A couple of times that night I had rolled over and fallen out of bed onto the concrete floor. I remembered nothing of this, but when I awoke the next morning and went into the shower, I caught a glimpse of my face in the mirror. I looked like I had been in a fist fight and had certainly been the loser! There was a nasty bruise with an abrasion on my head, both eyes were black, my whole face was swollen and bruised, and I had a good cut on my fat upper lip. "What in the hell happened?" I inquired of McKissick.

Shrugging his shoulders, he replied, "You fell out of bed several times. Your bunk mates kept putting you back in."

"Why didn't they just leave me on the floor?" I thought. My verbal retort is not printable.

I remember an incident following another detail I was on outside of the high walls of Bilibid. I don't remember the actual detail, but when I returned after a hard day's work in the heat, I enjoyed a cool, refreshing shower. I was in the process of getting dressed when a captain I did not know came in. He eyed me suspiciously and demanded to know what my rank was. When I told him I was a corporal he demanded to know why I was using the officer's shower. I told him I always used this particular facility. Furthermore, I was authorized to be there. He proceeded to kick me out with the admonition not to use it again. I was furious and said so in no uncertain terms.

When I talked to Major Wilson about the incident, he told me he had explained to the captain about the mix up and I could forget about the whole thing. What I did not previously know was that a change had been made while I was out on the detail, and the enlisted man's shower had been moved elsewhere. The one I just used was indeed an officer's shower. This was not the last time I would have a run-in with this officer.

As I stated earlier, food was becoming more scarce but the work details went on. There were several more bouts of malaria which tended to weaken me and my weight loss continued.

There was a red-headed Pharmacist Mate who worked in the kitchen and would smuggle extra rations of food in to me when I was ill. I'm sure his efforts in my behalf while putting his own safety at risk was a factor in keeping me on the "working well" list. I was shocked when I looked into a mirror and discovered I looked just about like the rest of the prisoners—thin, tired and listless. At least I was still among the "working well" and not bed-ridden like a good share of them were.

There must have been prisoners who were much more hungry than I because one morning the following notice was posted on the bulletin board:

MILITARY PRISON CAMP NO. 2 OF THE
PHILIPPINE ISLANDS, MANILA PI
January 9, 1945.
MEMORANDUM FOR ALL WARD SURGEONS
AND BUILDING LEADERS:

1. The following memorandum will be read to all personnel in your building at evening Tenko[56] this day then posted on Bulletin Boards:

Patients from Wards 1, 2, and 3 this morning were seen to be eating garbage that had been designated for the pigs. This trash is contaminated and may cause a fatal type of food poisoning. All personnel are forbidden from handling or eating garbage at any time.[57]

Warren A. Wilson, Major
Senior Medical Officer

There were a lot of pigeons that flew over the walls into the courtyard of Bilibid and they walked around pecking in the dirt looking for something to eat. Several of us decided a pigeon would make a nice addition to the skimpy rice meal if we could just corner and kill one of them. Lots of energy and effort was spent throwing sticks, rocks and anything else we hoped might injure a bird to a point we could catch it. The pigeons always

---

56. Morning and evening head count.
57. Copy of Memorandum on bulletin board at Bilibid Wendell brought home with him.

won the game of catch-me-if-you can and flew away mocking and jeering. We were never able to come close to injuring any of them, let alone cooking and eating one of the pesky birds.

We were hearing more good rumors all the time. Another secreted radio kept us informed and we knew General McArthur had landed on Leyte Island several hundred miles south of Manila. We also heard American forces had landed at the Lingayan Gulf on Luzon Island.

Occasionally we heard gunfire. As the days came and went, planes, all of them American, flew overhead. The terrific noise was music to our ears. We all knew liberation was coming and the anticipation of that glorious day kept us in good spirits. We did what we had to for survival.

> Work details were formed and sent out every day, manned mostly by the least sick, but many times those guys became more ill and were helped back by buddies who literally saved their lives. Without their aid they would have been left behind to die. Bodies got weaker and the deaths continued to climb.[58]

Sometime in late January, 1945 a group of women prisoners were brought into Bilibid from Santa Tomas University. They had been held there since the fall of Manila. Some of them were army nurses, some civilians, many of them with children. Most were emaciated from starvation and some were very ill. Among them was Elizabeth Golley, a twenty-something, rather attractive, protestant missionary who had been in China with her missionary parents when she was captured. She was one of the first white civilian women we had seen in a very long time.

She looked good to me, even though her tall frame was extremely thin, and she was in very poor health. She told us while she was a prisoner in Santa Tomas, even though they could see banana trees loaded with fat, ripe fruit outside the fence, the prisoners were not allowed to pick any of them. They were literally starving to death. But they were being denied food they could see, which undoubtedly would have relieved

---

58. McGarry talk, Memorial Day, Ephraim, Utah, 1997.

the hunger pangs and perhaps prevented death. They too had suffered mental as well as physical torture.

Elizabeth and I talked frequently and in the short time before I left Bilibid we became friends. We corresponded several times after the war. Then time, space and civilian life took over and we lost track of each other. But I have pleasant memories of that brief encounter so long ago with someone who had suffered the privations of life in a Japanese prison camp. She was very sick, she had experienced pain, and she had been extremely hungry; she understood.

At this time the daily food rations dropped dramatically. We were allowed one hundred grams of rice, and occasionally twenty grams of corn, per day, which when boiled in water, amounted to one canteen cup. Barely enough nourishment to sustain life, let alone supply energy and strength enough to work. Another one of the Navy Chiefs I knew had access to some additional food and he occasionally gave me his portion of rice. I don't know where his cache was or how he came by it and I didn't ask. I was just grateful to him for the extra rations.

Saturday, February 3, 1945, after almost three years of agonizing wondering, hoping, and waiting, we knew that the American troops had finally come into Manila. Even inside the high, thick walls of Bilibid Prison, all we could see was sky, but we could hear gunfire, thunderous explosions, and the unmistakable whine of American tank motors as they lumbered through the streets.

Monday, February 5th, the bombs and shells came very close. "Amid the confusion of the prisoners shouting for joy, running aimlessly to and fro in celebration, without any violent actions at all, the dazed Japanese guards just left. It became comparatively quiet except for the muffled sounds of war outside the walls of Bilibid."[59]

Then the gates opened. Trucks rolled into the prison courtyard carrying American soldiers. They were members of the United States Army 1st Cavalry. They were young, they were healthy, and we had waited a whole lifetime for them to come and get

59. Ibid.

us! Many of these young men shouted greetings as they leaped from the trucks with vigorous handshakes and hugs for the delighted prisoners. Others stared in stunned, horrified silence at the sight of us. We appeared as old men with matted beards and long dirty hair whose emaciated bodies were barely covered in filthy rags. Liberator tears flowed freely that fateful day and mingled with those of the liberated.

My heart was filled to overflowing with amazement and total disbelief that the day we had waited for an eternity to arrive was here at last. An indescribable feeling of relief and gratitude consumed me. Along with everyone else I wept the tears of a free man and sobbed my joyful thanksgiving to my Heavenly Father. I still cry when I think about it.

The prison gates were wide open.

> We were free! Some of us walked cautiously outside, just stood and stared around. Others of us ran, into the sweetest smelling air, a damp cloudy day and to the damnedest destruction we had ever seen! Nothing was left standing nearby, but a shoe factory and a brewery. Soldiers aren't stupid, they always know where the alcoholic beverages are, and they took advantage of the opportunity![60]

Three days later on February 8th the letter I wrote to my parents said:

> Dearest mother and dad,

> I can't begin to tell you my feelings upon seeing the old "yanks and tanks." Let alone how happy being free and able to write-actually write you my parents that I'm free. The nearest this feeling comes to is like a small child seeing their first Christmas tree, or something like that. Anyway it's a great feeling!

---

60. McGarry talk, Ephraim, 1994.

– 10 –

FREEDOM AT LAST!

Evacuation of the women and children prisoners who came from Santa Tomas was done first. There were suspicions that the prison was mined with explosives as the Japanese Commander had been ordered to kill all of the prisoners. We heard this death rumor at Cabanatuan and it was noised about at Bilibid as well. No one knew for sure that the mining had not been done, so they were loaded onto the trucks and taken out to the safety of the shoe factory.

The next day more trucks were loaded with the patients in the hospital who were seriously ill, many of them near death. I was one of the working well who was designated to go along as caregiver for a load of these very sick people. Preparations to leave Bilibid and eventual loading of the patients had taken most of the daylight hours.

Fighting in areas of Manila as well as the surrounding area was still hot and heavy. The soldier driving our truck was completely unfamiliar with the area, and we became lost several times, finding ourselves dangerously close to the ongoing battle fronts. Numerous times we were directed back to roads that would eventually lead us to the Lingayan Gulf which was a rest camp for the liberated prisoners.

It was between 2 and 3 o'clock in the morning before we arrived. Even in the pre-dawn darkness the whole camp was a beehive of activity. Everywhere American soldiers were unloading trucks assisting those who needed help, and I could smell the delicious aroma of cooking food. A well-stocked kitchen was set up and open for business twenty-four hours a day.

The truck on which I was riding stopped. Immediately, I was invited to get off and let the soldiers wearing medic insignias on their uniforms take over the unloading of the patients. I stepped to the rear of the vehicle and was ready to climb down when a stocky built soldier, probably in his mid thirties, extended his hand, smiled at me and exclaimed, "Come on, Mac, let me give you a hand."

I refused with, "Thanks. I can manage."

He reached up—not too gently—took hold of my clothes and lifted me—all of my less-than-one-hundred pound—off the truck. Being tired, stressed, and hungry as hell, I was a little peeved, but when I read his name tag, "Sergeant Wendell Bunker," I forgot about being angry. Instead I said, "I'll be damned! My name is Wendell, Wendell H. McGarry. In fact my mother's brother, Uncle Othello Hickman, married a Helen Bunker."

Sergeant Bunker laughed out loud and said, "You've got to be kidding! Helen is my sister!"

There we were, two perfect strangers, thousands of miles from home, meeting under the most unusual of circumstances, feeling like long lost siblings getting together for the first time. I was deeply touched.

Almost instantly Wendell Bunker and I became dear friends. For the first time in more than three years since I had come to the Philippine Islands, I began to feel connected to the United States, to Utah, to family. We formed a bond that would become strong enough to endure through the years, through time and space to the end of our lives.

I was taken to the kitchen and invited to have anything to eat or drink I desired. I asked for a drink of pineapple juice. In holding the cup of coveted yellow liquid in my hand and inhaling the delicious smell of the fruit, I knew I was not dreaming. Everything happening around me was in fact, pure reality. I tasted, then drank deeply, draining the cup. In a matter of minutes, I passed out. My poor emaciated body was unable to assimilate the sugar; graphic effects of severe malnutrition.

I completely enjoyed my first leisurely hot shower since before the war on Corregidor with soap and a clean fresh smelling towel, plus a shave and a long overdue GI haircut. It seemed to have been a whole lifetime since theses simple, yet wonderful, rituals I had taken so for granted had occurred.

We were issued clean, fresh, completely whole clothing, underwear, suntan shirts, and pants. For the last time, my mother's beautiful gold wedding band was unpinned and taken out of my pants waist band where it had been hidden for almost three years. It slid easily onto my little finger where it still fit. I was actually taking it home to my Mother.

Then the rags I had been wearing were tossed, along with those of the other POWs, onto a smoldering fire. Socks and real leather shoes were issued to us. Shoes felt really "funny." After literally years of wearing the dirty, smelly wooden clogs we had made ourselves out of pieces of wood with straps over the toes, it would take some time getting used to the confining GI shoes. The wonder of all that was happening to me was overwhelming.

I am not sure just how long we stayed at Lingayan, a week, perhaps longer. All I remember for sure is that we had all we wanted to eat, sometimes enough to make us sick. Then we ate again. For the first time in almost three dreadful years the hunger we had endured, had lived with and from which so many had died, was finally being satisfied.

We were also allowed to rest and relax. No more endless exhausting work details. We slept at first uneasily on army cots with clean sheets, pillows, and new blankets. It was almost too much to comprehend.

All of us gained weight rapidly. Very quickly my belt tightened and I had to make it larger. The absolute total joy I felt nearly consumed me.

I visited with Wendell Bunker briefly and we talked about our families at home. He told me of his beloved wife Marian and his small daughter Susan. He gave me money and asked when I returned home if I would buy a little doll and send it to Susan for her birthday in April. He was sure he would not be home by that time. There was much more work for him to do. After emotional good-byes were said and we hugged, my new found friend, my hero, was gone.

Our time at the Lingayan Gulf rest camp was coming to an end and liberated prisoners were being shipped out by air to

Leyte Island where General McArthur made his return landing in October 1944. I was flown with a load of the prisoners who had gained weight and enough strength to travel to Tacloban, the capital city of Leyte. There we were to board ships to sail back home to America to dock in San Francisco. It seemed to me everything was moving in slow motion. I was so anxious to get on that ship and go home. Then the unthinkable happened.

Several days before we were to board the ship and get under way I became very ill. I developed a terrific pain in my gut, specifically in the lower right quadrant. On examination at the base hospital, the doctor diagnosed the pain as a possible appendicitis. However, I had no elevated temperature or white blood cell count, so I was given pain medication, sedated, and put to bed. A doctor would check with me in the morning.

I was no stranger to pain. Enduring rib-cracking kicks and slaps so hard I nearly blacked out had hardened me. The excruciating pain of a Japanese rifle butt that could unexpectedly connect with any part of my body had made me familiar with the concept of being beaten to the point of unconsciousness. I'd nearly starved to death, but this searing pain in my gut was the final straw. I couldn't take any more to body or soul. Was this to be the final extraction of one more pound of flesh?

I had waited so long to be liberated from the hell of prison camp I could hardly contain myself. Desperately yearning to go home to America, I hated the mysterious malady that delayed my homecoming. Preparations for sailing were under way. The ship was being loaded but I would not be on it. Confined to bed in a military hospital still on the Island of Leyte, in the Philippine Islands, restlessly waiting for the relief that a shot of morphine and a sleeping pill could give me, I cursed my bad luck. But the aching disappointment and yearning for home in my heart would not go away. The medication was casting its spell and as I floated into the drug induced slumber my last lucid thought was, "Damn the pain! Damn this rotten war! I want to go home!"

It must have been near midnight or a little later I felt someone gently shaking me, pleading, cajoling, "Mac, wake up! Can you hear me? Come on buddy, wake up, we're going to get you out of here!"

Opening my eyes, I peered through the fog of pain and sleeping meds slowly recognizing the fuzzy image that appeared. I felt the rapid breathing of the face almost touching mine and I could tell that it was my dentist friend Dr. McKissick in a hospital garb. His was the voice that whispered me into consciousness while I struggled to collect my senses. He continued to whisper, encouraging me to stay awake, but to be quiet in the process.

In the dim light I could see that there were a couple more hospital uniformed shadows standing by my bed. Strong arms quietly lifted me onto a litter and quickly carried me out of the hospital. That is all I remember of that night.

I awakened the next morning to the pulsating sound of motors and the swaying of the ship. Dr. McKissick was standing at my bedside to answer the questions of "Where am I, and how in the hell did I get here?"

"After all we've been through together, you really didn't think we'd go home without you, did you?" he quietly replied.

****

It must have taken several days for the *USS AE Anderson*[61] troop ship to get us to Hollandia, New Guinea. Up to that time I wasn't even sure what ship I was on. All I really cared about was that we were on our way home. Nothing else mattered. Our stay in Hollandia was brief, perhaps a couple of days. By this time I was virtually pain free and able to eat almost anything. I could hardly believe anytime I wanted to, I could eat and there was plenty of everything.

A couple of instances come to mind as I reflect upon that final voyage home. One day I was sprinting up the stairway on my way to the upper deck to visit with one of my officer friends when I almost ran into a captain coming down the steps toward me. I stepped back, attempting to apologize, then I recognized the arrogant S.O.B. who had kicked me out of the officers' shower in Bilibid. Recognition registered in his eyes almost simultaneously. Something like the following verbal

---

61. The *USS General AE Anderson* was a Liberty Ship originally built as a transport vessel. It was converted to bring the POWs home from the Pacific Theatre of war after the Philippines were liberated.

confrontation followed, "Corporal, get the hell out of my way," the captain demanded.

"Kiss my ass," the cocky corporal retorted as he not too gently brushed past the livid officer and continued the sprint up the stairs.

Instinctively, I knew I would be hearing from Major Wilson soon and I probably deserved a reprimand. But he was used to settling these kinds of childish disputes and he was in no mood for a big deal. He merely restricted me to my deck for the rest of the voyage. With a twinkle in his tired eyes he told me the captain had been restricted to his deck as well. Justice had been satisfied.

Occasionally this very matter was referred to in a joking way in the Christmas greetings that Major Wilson and I exchanged after my graduation from dental school and several years into my practice. If I didn't mention it, he would.

I also remember the good looking American woman who was probably thirty something and who looked much better in every way than any of the other women prisoners from Santa Tomas. She was not as thin from lack of food or nutrition. In fact she looked healthy, she was comparatively well dressed but the look in her eyes was full of sadness and pain. She was traveling with two beautiful young children. A Caucasian boy, perhaps six years old, who looked much like his mother and another handsome little boy, probably close to two years old, whose almond shaped eyes and jet black hair were unmistakably Oriental.

I have always enjoyed children, regardless of their race or color. I found it an easy, very pleasant thing to engage in small talk with the lady after making friends with her children. After several conversations, she told me that she and her three year old son had been captured after her husband, an American officer, was killed in Manila. They were taken to Santa Tomas where they very nearly starved to death. In order to protect her son and obtain food for him, she seduced a Japanese officer and became his mistress. He treated her with a degree of respect, kindness, and even love. Eventually she bore him a son. He was killed when the Americans liberated the city.

She confided her deep concern for her second child. How would he be received in America? Even by her parents, her siblings? If it was her fate to be ostracized for her flagrant collaboration with the enemy, so be it. She was terribly haunted by the fact that through this collaboration she had averted the possible death of one child, but in doing so had she condemned a second innocent to an existence of persecution, discrimination, and torment in the American society where they were to live? I sensed her desperation and I hope I may have contributed a little to her peace of mind when I told her that all of us did the best we could. Considering the circumstances of the war, we did what we hoped was right. Only time and distance from the hell we had lived as POWs and the actions we had taken would tell if we were right or not. We did what we had to do. I wished her well when we said goodbye, and have since wondered how things went for her and for her two charming little sons.

It seemed to me that we had been at sea for a dreadfully long period of time, probably because we were in waters still full of hostile and extremely dangerous Japanese submarines. The war was not over for the U.S. and her allies and would not reach a successful victorious conclusion until August 1945 after the detonation of the atomic bombs on two Japanese cities.

The ship's captain had ordered the navigational officers to maintain a zigzag pattern of travel which considerably slowed our progress. Upon inquiry, I was told it took a submarine about the same period of time to get an accurate reading on a ship as it did for the vessel to zigzag, just a couple of minutes, making it much less likely to fire a torpedo with successful accuracy.

I remember standing on deck at the stern of the ship in the light of the moon watching the weird looking wake trailing behind as the big vessel turned this way and that. For some very strange reason the foamy columns reminded me of the Wasatch mountain range surrounding the Salt Lake Valley covered in snow during the Utah winter.

The voyage was much slower than I would have liked, but I took advantage of the time period to rest, to read, and to listen to some of the Big Band music that had become popular while I was gone. I was amazed at some of the nonsensical things that I heard, for instance: *The Three Little Fishes*, which went something like this:

Down in the meadow in the itty, bitty pool
fam fee litty fitty, and the Mama fitty too,
Fim said the Mama fitty, fim if you can
and they fam and they fam all over the dam!
Boop, boop, dittum, dattum, wattum, choo!
(repeat)
And they fam and they fam all over the dam."[62]

I couldn't believe it! I wondered if the American society as a whole had deteriorated in a like manner!

I spent considerable time eating and gaining more pounds. By the time I arrived home I would be ten pounds away from my normal weight, feeling good and looking more like my pre-war self. I would dream of seeing my family again, of the girl I left behind in 1941 who promised to wait for my return. A faint hope persisted that she was still waiting as I had not heard from her since before the fall of Corregidor. I knew the four years we had been separated was a long time to expect anyone as young and lovely as she was to stay single. I was hoping for the best, yet sort of preparing for the worst.

We had been sailing for more than twenty days, a much longer time to return home than it had been to get to the Philippines in 1941. But I was going the right way this time, I was going home!

There was a period of time that the *AE Anderson* had run into some very unsettling weather. I felt once more the dizziness and the nausea creep upward into my throat as the big ship lumbered up and down, smacking hard on the flat bottom, sidewise, backward, then forward again. I remembered my vow as I suffered the same symptoms while traveling to the Philippines. "I would never get on another ship, only the one that was taking me back to the United States!" Even though it was uncomfortable, to say the least, it didn't seem to matter quite so much.

We sailed up the fog enshrouded coast of California, the deck railings of the ship packed with anxious, eager, homesick Americans, peering into the fog, straining to catch a glimpse of

---

62. Originally recorded by the "Smoothies", Victor Records, March, 1939.

familiarity. Suddenly, as if a giant door opened, there she was, the Golden Gate Bridge in all her majestic glory, stretching her arms across San Francisco Bay to welcome us home. Once more the overwhelming emotions of the spirit of freedom, gratitude, love of family, home, and country engulfed me. My tears of joyful disbelief mingled once more with those of my fellow POWs. It was March 8, 1945.

As the *AE Anderson* glided closer to the bridge we could see literally thousands of people standing on it. They were waving flags, hats, and scarves, with arms outstretched, hands beckoning to us as if to hasten the arrival of the ship and her precious cargo. And they were screaming ecstatically! The scene beneath her wide expanse was one of organized chaos. Literally hundreds of boats jammed the harbor, fog horns blaring. Air raid sirens screamed their welcome. Fire boats spewed fluffy white columns of water high into the air. Overhead, numerous aircraft thundered their welcome. Thousands of adoring Americans lined the wharf, adding to the welcome celebration with their cheers, whistles, and just plain yelling. Bands played, people laughed and shouted greetings through their tears. It was wonderful! San Francisco had gone all out to welcome home the first returning POWs from the Pacific Theatre of war. Silently we wept our thanks and appreciation. Awaking from the dreams we had nurtured of returning home was sweet to the taste, yet bitter to the memory of those who were left behind never to return.

I don't have the words to fully describe the feelings in my heart at the precious moment, but I had never known the joy, the pure love of God and of my country that were mine at that time. Never before or since! The excited apprehension and wariness I felt mounting inside me as we drew near to American soil had somehow melted away, leaving me with a sense of peace of mind and spirit that I had not felt in years. As understanding filled my heart at the joyous display of loyal concern and love our America was demonstrating for us, the feelings of loneliness and abandonment I felt when we were captured dissipated. Love pushed the bitterness out of my heart. Humility and gratitude took its place.

After the *Anderson* was coaxed to the pier by the little tug boats and the gang plank let down, family members and well wishers edged closer to get the first look at the returnees. As the POWs, military personnel, and civilians who were aboard ship walked down the gangplank, recognition of a loved one set off another explosion of screams, hugs, kisses, and tears.

There were those who, when their feet touched American soil, fell to their knees and kissed the ground. This action elicited another roar of approval from the crowd. I felt the same way but I didn't like the possibility that I could be overrun in the process so I resisted the temptation.

I was fairly certain that none of my immediate family would be waiting for me, as Utah was not close. Although they had been notified by telegram I was on my way home, I was not sure they had been informed as to the specific date and time of my arrival. What I wanted most at that moment was to get to a telephone. I gave my parents a call that night after waiting in line for what seemed an eternity. It was 1:30 before I was able to get through to Salt Lake City. My Mother in was in tears. "Oh, my son, my son! Thank you God, for bringing him home," she sobbed.

I was beginning to feel I really was home. I could hear the relief in her voice. I told her I was fine and I would let them know later when I would be returning home to Utah. At the time my dad was working in Hanford, Washington. I would see him when he arrived in Salt Lake City.

Buses were waiting for us. It took a considerable amount of time to load the vehicles, get us on our way to the Presidio and eventually to Lettermans Hospital. We were to be quarantined for twenty-four hours to be examined from head to toe, prodded, poked, and tested for the presence of parasites. Blood, urine and fecal samples were taken and tested to make sure that we were not bringing home a myriad of tropical diseases. Doctors and female nurses were doing the work. They may have been looking at us but we did our share of staring as well.

I was once more entertaining some painful sensations in my right side although not as severe as it had been on Leyte. So I became a patient at Letterman to undergo more observation.

Later, I was glad for the time in the hospital, which gave me a while to recover from the news from my mother that my special girl had not waited. She had married in 1943 after I was declared missing in action. I was not too surprised. I had hoped that she would wait, but for nearly four years? My eventual understanding and acceptance of the time, the distance factors, and not knowing of my fate made things a little easier for me to accept.

I received a degree of comfort in the fact that I had kept our relationship close to my heart all through prison camp. It had been a strong incentive to fight the battle to survive. For that I was grateful, but the sting of loneliness and hurt remained. No definite diagnosis of my pain was ever made by the MDs. I was eventually given a clean bill of health, released from the hospital, and sent back to the Presidio to my outfit.

During the next couple of weeks, we were interviewed countless times by government and Red Cross representatives. Military people and social workers were present to get personal histories of our confinement as POWs. I was sure that a lot of unnecessary information was being pried out of us, but we were still members of the military and we did what we were told, like it or not.

We had each received a letter from President Roosevelt welcoming us home and we were later entertained by Eddie Cantor, a most amusing comic and singer. The Mayor of San Francisco presented us with a key to the city which gave us lots of free privileges. We also received medallions entitling us to ride free in taxi cabs. We were treated like royalty and we loved every minute of it! We were wined and dined, entertained by movie stars, and made to feel very special about returning home from the war. We were all regarded as heroes and it made us feel good.

Several of the guys aboard the *Anderson* and I were invited by Mario Machi, one of our Italian XPOW friends who lived in San Francisco, to a dinner which his family held to celebrate his homecoming. His father purchased an expensive bottle of wine before he left for the Philippine Islands and it was put in the wine cellar until Mario returned from active duty. It was to finally be used to welcome him home. The evening was well spent and we appreciated the warm friendly actions of the whole family toward us.

Several of the Navy Chiefs from Bilibid I knew hosted a celebration at a luxury hotel and a few of us were invited to the "Top of the Mark" to help them celebrate. Evidently, the suite they were using and the refreshments being served were courtesy of several wealthy people, including some movie stars, who were anxious to show their appreciation to POWs. They told us they had been there for several days and they would go home when the liquor ran out.

In 1941, prior to my departure for the Philippines and while I was at Fort McDowell, I had gotten a pass and visited my Uncle George and his family in San Francisco. His daughter, my cousin Mary Lou, had introduced me to her girlfriend and I promised I would call her on my return. Of course she was expecting that I would be home in two years and so was I. After calling her I was surprised she was still available so we made a date. But it was not to be.

The evening I was getting ready to pick her up to go dancing an announcement came over the intercom, "Sergeant McGarry, your mother is waiting for you in the lobby." I was so excited to see my Mom. I thanked my Heavenly Father for taking care of her while I was away for so long. The tenderness I felt for my beloved Mother overflowed in my heart and my tears of love and gratitude mingled with hers.

I never did get to see the girl again. A couple of days later, my Mother and I boarded a United Airliner to make the last lap of my long journey home. (Mom's ticket cost $33.60. My ticket was supplied by the military.)[63]

We landed at the Salt Lake City International Airport on March 26, 1945, where, to my surprise, we were met by a huge number of my immediate and extended family, friends, and neighbors. They shouted their greetings with smiles and tears. There were hugs and more tears. The media was there with cameras flashing and questions flying.

"Sergeant McGarry, how does it feel to be home?" "What are

---

63. Receipt for Mother's flight on United Airlines March 26, 1945.

your plans? Will you stay in Salt Lake City? Will you go back to school?"

It was great! As I looked around the beautiful Salt Lake Valley after four very long years away from all that was familiar to me, it was a sweet, humbling experience to finally be back home where I belonged.

– 11 –

MORE PROBLEMS

We came home to America. We thought our troubles were all over. We rushed into the areas we wanted to pursue—school, jobs, marriage and rearing of families. But new ordeals surfaced. We discovered life at home was not what we expected. Things had changed. We were different. Some of us faced extreme difficulty in adjusting to every-day civilian life. We couldn't sleep. Nightmares haunted us. We constantly lived in the past and we wondered if living was worth the struggle.[64]

It was not worth it to some of us. Suicide became the most common cause of death among newly returned POWs. A gun was the easiest, fastest way to curtail the continual flow of nightmares, the constant nagging of fearful reactions to the peal of thunder or the pop of a firecracker. The mere sight of a firearm of any caliber struck instant terror to my heart. My fear was that, perhaps, I could not resist the temptation to use it. I stayed completely away from weapons of any kind.

When the screaming would awaken her or the late night touch of my Mother tucking the covers around my shoulders would bring me upright, wild-eyed and spewing forth expletives, I began to realize that though the physical circumstances and surroundings of my life were different, nothing else had really changed. The deep-seated fears, insecurity, and loneliness I had experienced in prison camp were still embedded firmly into my mind.

64. McGarry talk. Ephraim, Utah, 1994.

My only refuge became a bottle of whiskey. I sipped on one during the day. I had one sitting on the night stand at my bedside. The alcohol and the numbing effect it had on me was blessed relief from the nagging pain I carried with me for so long. The liquor became an obsession.

I discovered I was not alone in these negative feelings. Robert Strasters, the O.R. technician from Salt Lake City I met in the hospital at Cabanatuan, arrived home just before I did. We contacted each other almost immediately. Bob often called me, his voice trembling with desperation. His thoughts of suicide were becoming so strong he really feared what he might do. We talked on the phone, sometimes for hours and frequently into the middle of the night, stopping only when one of us asked, "Are you going to be all right?" And the other one would answer in the affirmative. I did my share of contacting him as well. We met often, always in a public place, a coffee house or bar and the discussions resumed, for hours and hours. We literally saved each other's lives on numerous occasions. This interaction continued for months.

Then I received a disturbing telephone call from my quan buddy Everett Turney. He was in a state of disbelief and pain. His mother had passed away while we were gone and his dad had remarried. When he went back to Texas to live, his dad and stepmother had not been able to cope with the same kind of things my parents were suffering through. Could he come to Utah and spend some time with me?

I consulted my mother about Everett coming to visit. She reluctantly agreed. Almost from the beginning after his arrival, the drinking increased since there were two of us involved. A short while later, Mother asked me to take my friend and find another place to stay. My older brother Derrell and his wife lived in a house with an unfinished basement and they invited us stay with them for a while.

Everett eventually went back to Texas. I went home, continued drinking, and embarrassing my Mother. On one occasion that I am certainly not proud of, Mom was enjoying a late afternoon visit with a couple of neighbor ladies in the living room. I had just showered and was probably plowed by that late hour in the day. I had not bothered to get dressed. I was wearing just a towel around my waist when I walked into the room where the three very shocked ladies gaped at me. I greeted them politely and continued into the bedroom. Mother was horrified by the blatant, disrespectful display and she let me know about it in no uncertain terms. I felt no shame or anger, and certainly no pleasure for my actions. I simply didn't care.

The vice-principle, Miss Dyer of South High School where I graduated in 1937, had taken a special interest in me when I was a student. After reading the newspaper about my return home from prison camp, she invited me to come and talk to a student body assembly about my experiences. I refused to talk to the kids but I did agree to speak to the faculty. The only thing I really remember about the incident was being extremely uncomfortable recalling some of the things they wanted to hear and the way I delivered the talk. I could not stand still. I found myself nervously pacing back and forth across the stage in the auditorium, talking incessantly while smoking a cigarette.

Another incident that occurred during this same period of time has now given me additional insight into the twisted state of my mind. My older brother Chauncy was a Salt Lake City police officer. He was going on a detail in the city to pick up a prisoner and he invited me to go along. I can remember vividly how I felt when he told the prisoner if he even thought about escaping, I had been a prisoner of war and I would not think twice about killing him for any stupid thing he might try. I was horrified when I realized that I could have done exactly as my brother said with no feelings of remorse or guilt. Even though I was no longer in a war and had no reason to defend myself, it didn't seem to matter. I could easily have shot the man and not cared one way or the other. My thinking was flawed, my emotions were dormant, and it frightened me.

These things happened just a short time before my trip to Lake Placid, N.Y. for R and R. In retrospect, this journey across the United States on a train and the experiences I had during that time would prove to be positive profound elements in the healing process which would eventually lead me back into the realm of near normalcy.

JOYCE

In the letter dated May 3, 1942, the last one written to my folks before the fall of the Philippine Islands, I sent $80 in Philippine pesos home to my mother. Luckily, I was able to send it out from Corregidor with an army nurse. Corregidor fell to the Japanese three days later, on May 6, 1942.

Of course, after the fall, Philippine pesos were no longer considered legal tender, but Mother assumed the army should make the exchange as these pesos were my last pay before the fall. She wrote several letters to different government agencies attempting to accomplish this, but to no avail.

After I arrived back in Salt Lake City, I went to Fort Douglas to see if I could get the paymaster there to make the trade. I was directed to the colonel in charge of Finance and Travel who assured me that I could not convert the pesos into American dollars. Being very short on patience and having zero tolerance for what I viewed as incompetence, I told him in no uncertain terms, using every "Old Army" expletive at my disposal what I thought of the whole situation and of him in particular.

Being red of face but possessing an uncanny ability to control his temper, he quietly but firmly said, "Young man just who do you think you are? You can't talk that way to a colonel. And if you were anyone but a POW I would have your ass thrown in the stockade and I would personally throw away the damn key!" Looking me straight in the eye, even more calmly he continued,

"However, in light of the circumstances I believe that the Army does owe you some reimbursement. All POWs are entitled to be reimbursed for everything they lost when they were captured. The money is to come from Japanese assets in the United States which were frozen just after Pearl Harbor. You are also entitled to a month of R and R. Just give me a list of all of the items you lost when you were captured, including the eighty pesos which would have exchanged for $40 U.S. dollars."

After I completed the list he asked where I preferred to go for my month of R and R. I had no idea until he listed the places from which I could choose. These included among others, Los Angeles, Miami, and Lake Placid, New York. By this time I had calmed down enough to hear and fully understand what he was saying. I suppose I may have offered something that was close to an apology. I then told him I had a sister and her family in Schenectady, New York. If it could be arranged, I would like to spend several days with them as well as some time with a boyhood buddy stationed at an army base near Rock Island, Illinois. Lake Placid, New York was my choice for two weeks of R and R. I left the colonel's office with his assurance that final arrangements would be made and I would receive notification very soon. It was the middle of June when I received train tickets as well as spending money and my reservations at Lake Placid.

I caught the eastbound train at Union Station in Salt Lake City. In a few hours I arrived in Denver where I spent the day sightseeing, after which I boarded the train for an overnight trip to Rock Island, Illinois on the banks of the Mississippi River. I was met at the train station by my friend Frank Nesbitt's wife Norma, who informed me Frank had left that morning on a special mission and wasn't expected back until the day that I was to leave to continue my trip to New York State.

I had no choice but to spend the next few days with Norma and her more than willing neighbor girl. We ate out, renewed our friendship and we played a hell of a round of golf on a course that was located on a sand bar in the Mississippi River. I had regained the strength in my body and was feeling pretty much back to normal. Maybe it helped to be able to impress the girls, but I was hitting the ball three hundred yards and was making some pro-like putts, which added up to a terrific game. The golf pro was playing ahead of us but he insisted we play through. I was completely enjoying myself.

The morning I was to leave came all too quickly. I reluctantly bid Norma good-bye at the train station, all the while lamenting the fact that I had missed spending some good time with Frank. She was to pick him up at the station that evening. Of course we gave the neighbors some food for thought and some basis for juicy gossip about Norma entertaining a strange soldier while her soldier husband was away on assignment.

My next stop was at Schenectady, New York where I spent a most enjoyable time with my sister Fern and her husband Burt. It was good to see their children and to get acquainted with their three-year-old son who was born in 1942 about the time I was declared missing in action. They named him Wendell and he was a very special nephew. I stayed several days then continued on my way to New York City.

When I arrived at Union Station in New York City, which during the war was an extremely busy place, I was able to hail a taxi and asked the driver to take me to the Taft Hotel. After several minutes of driving around the busy streets, we pulled up in front of the hotel. As I paid for the cab, I looked across the street and there was Union Station. The driver was grinning as he took the money from this very obviously inexperienced country boy who was anything but happy about having been "taken" so soon in the big city. I stayed in the overcrowded, dirty city whose streets were saturated with panhandlers for a couple of days, then caught a train to Lake Placid.

The Lake Placid Club, which is located in the Adirondack Mountain region of New York State on the shores of Mirror Lake, was designated as a Redistribution Station. Returnees from the war fronts were sent here to be reevaluated and studied as to their physical and mental conditions. They were then reassigned to areas where they would be most useful to the army for the duration of the war.[65] However, I was not a part of the redistribution process. I was there solely to "rest and relax."

---

65. Lake Placid Club booklet distributed by the Special Service Command to all military personnel who came for R and R.

I was shown to my assigned room in the huge, beautiful Lake Placid Club where I was to be a guest of the army for two weeks. I was invited to use any and all of the facilities for my comfort and enjoyment the club had offered its many wealthy patrons for the previous fifty years.

I mentioned earlier ever since returning home from prison camp, my nights were filled with haunting nightmares and in all of my waking hours visions of the extremely traumatic experiences which I lived for three years lingered just below the surface of my mind. I found the only way to dull the unpleasant memories was with alcohol. A fifth of whiskey became my best friend. When I awoke from a particularly gruesome nightmare at home my mother would come in to see what the screaming was all about. I asked her to leave me alone, sometimes not too nicely. Once again I took solace in the security of the bottle. Then and only then did I find a very temporary, somewhat troubled peace.

The first day, July 5th, I awoke early, walked the few steps outside my ground floor room, and dove into the deserted swimming pool. While doing a few laps, I found myself reviving as the cool water enveloped and invigorated me. After a good breakfast of pancakes, bacon and eggs in the dining room, I took my golf clubs and played a round or two. The remainder of the day was spent getting acquainted with my surroundings and beginning another fifth of whiskey.

When the heat of the day melted into evening and I had finished dinner, I walked over to the Copacetic[66] Day and Night Club. Twice a week, dozens of enlisted men danced the night away to the popular Big Band sound of the Special Service Band. The gals who came by the bus load from New York City were mostly college girls and a welcome addition to the resort. As I mounted the steps, I saw the shadow of a young woman standing on the porch. She seemed to be alone. I spoke to her and we talked for a while before she consented to go inside and dance.

As I held this warm petite female in my arms and looked into her soft brown eyes, I sensed a very special relationship

66. Webster defines copacetic as meaning good, excellent, or fine.

was about to begin. Her first name was Joyce and her surname, along with the shining black hair that cascaded to her shoulders and curled softly around her pretty face, were strong indicators of her Jewish blood.

She was nineteen and a student at exclusive Endicott College located in Beverly, Massachusetts. Her father was on Wall Street and they had a Park Avenue address. Good indications of wealth which definitely put her out of my social class. Somehow it didn't seem to matter.

Together we danced to the romantic melodies of the Big Band, all the while getting to know each other, asking and answering questions. We walked beneath the stars, we spoke of hopes and dreams, of life and of love. Much too soon the witching hour arrived and the bus was ready to leave for New York City. I kissed her a reluctant good-bye. With a promise to return the next day, she was gone.

As I walked back to my room I felt an emotional awakening deep within my heart. Feelings I feared had died while I was in prison camp had quickened. This lovely young woman awakened in me a renewed zest for life. I had the sensation of being reborn spiritually, mentally and emotionally. For the first time in more than three and one half years I felt in touch with reality. She was real. We were here together. The flame of emotions within me I long thought had been extinguished was glowing again and the warmth of joyful feeling once more filled my entire being.

During the night, my nightmares resumed their place in my psyche and I reached for the fifth of whiskey waiting to dull the pain and erase the horrific images. I finally succumbed to the effects of the liquor and fell into a fitful, restless slumber. Sleep and the liquor had a numbing effect on my body, and when I awakened early, I stumbled to the swimming pool and dove into the cool, refreshing water, descending clear to the bottom. And there I stayed! Try as I might I could not get up from the bottom of that pool. As I struggled, I felt my breath being depleted. My lungs were bursting and I was in prison camp again. I knew this time I was going to die!

Utter complete panic took custody of me. I struggled aimlessly, and if it had been possible, I would have cried out for help. Then

I felt the grip of a strong hand grasping mine. I was being pulled up toward the surface. As my face broke the water, the rush of fresh air into my burning lungs was instant release from the terror of helpless imprisonment. I was truly free again! I said a silent prayer of thanks as I turned to face my rescuer. A young soldier was walking away, dripping wet, and with the wave of a hand, he passed off my efforts to thank him. Then he was gone. I never did find out who he was or where he came from. Whether it was pure coincidence he should be at the pool-side at the moment when I desperately needed his help or whether it was once again divine intervention, for I had felt that influence before, I will never know. But I was very grateful.

Not only had the death of my physical body been prevented but something very positive happened in my psyche. I was now able to face the challenges of the continually returning prison camp experiences which were not only consuming my waking hours and disrupting my sleep, but were very nearly destroying me.

My obsession with alcohol had been satisfied and it was an easy thing for me to take my stash of liquor—a couple fifths of whiskey—out of my room and empty them onto the ground. Several other servicemen in the room next to mine who were standing nearby stood in stunned silence for a moment as they watched in horror. Then with cries of protest they begged me to stop. I could have given the liquor to them but I needed to destroy it. For me it was liberating therapy. It felt good to be rid of the dominance the alcohol had over me. I had just taken a giant step down the path toward healing. This process would be painfully slow and it would continue for years.

True to her word, Joyce returned the next day and the next and the next and for twelve more exciting days. I was in seventh heaven.

Her family owned a boat house (our whole house in Utah could have fit in the living room) on the lake where we spent many wonderful hours together, swimming, boating, exchanging information about each other on long walks as well as dancing at the club. I found peace and total contentment with Joyce.

An enjoyable date that stands out clearly in my memory was when we spent an evening at the club where Dean Martin and

Jerry Lewis were the guest performers. We completely enjoyed their antics as they bantered back and forth with insults and hilarious one-liners. I hadn't laughed like that in years. Then we basked in the spell of the romantic ballads as only Dean Martin could croon them.

It was on the third day I found myself waiting for Joyce at the boathouse when a limousine drove up. A well dressed gentleman accompanied by a hulking brute of a man with cauliflower ears and the neck of a bull stepped out of the car and came into the house. The gentleman introduced himself as Joyce's father. He proceeded to inform me in no uncertain terms if I were responsible for anything happening to his daughter with a violation of any kind, I could expect to be well taken care of by his henchman. And it wouldn't be pretty. He left no doubt whatsoever in my mind that it would happen.

His threats of physical violence made me angry and I told him if anything should happen to me there was a whole group of seasoned well-trained killers staying at the Lake Placid Club who would be more than happy to retaliate with violence of a special kind against him and his overgrown bodyguard. Nothing more needed to be said. I think we understood each other completely.

I had fallen deeply in love with this lovely girl. She represented all of the sweet relationships, the carefree experiences, the joys of young manhood I had not known while I lived through the hell of prison camp. I felt liberated. I was almost a whole human being again. She had given me back a segment of my life that had been denied me while my spirit as well as my body was in bondage. And I loved her for it.

My time in this heaven was rapidly coming to a close. One evening a sergeant came to me and explained that someone had rented a plane and several couples were flying to Vermont that evening to be married. Did Joyce and I want to go along? I was sorely tempted and I was sure she was willing. I had always planned to marry and give my bride the wedding ring that had belonged to my mother—the one I carried all through prison camp. Now it was in a drawer at home in Salt Lake City. Perhaps if it had been in my pocket things might have been different.

Then common sense took over and I considered the difference in our backgrounds and the cold hard fact that I had literally nothing to offer her but myself. I had no money, my education was not complete, the course of my life was uncertain. I was afraid it would not be enough for her—a girl raised with everything that money and social position could bring. And I was sure it would not be nearly enough for her father. Then I remembered his warning. Would marrying her be a violation in his eyes? There had been nothing to worry about to this point. Our relationship had been tender, pure and simple. I didn't even tell her about the invitation. I just said "no."

Our last goodbye on the 18th of July, 1945 was filled with tears. As we held each other close, promises of letters, telephone calls and plans were made for eventually meeting again. My heart was heavy as I boarded the train and headed west and home.

The next few months were indeed full of letters and phone calls. Almost every day for the first few weeks there was communication between us. As I went back to the University of Utah to school and she returned to the exclusive private school in Massachusetts, the intervals between the letters and the telephone calls increased. Time and distance were taking their toll on our relationship. Even after I was married, in dental school, and the father of two little blond daughters, there still remained in my heart deep feelings for this girl whose brief sojourn into my life was so meaningful. I heard from her several times, and the temptation to see her once more was difficult to resist. But I did. I have on occasion wondered "what if," and then the thought was put aside for the good life I was living.

Many times I tried to explain to my wife about my relationship with Joyce and what it had meant to me, but she was never quite able to understand.

– 13 –

AFTERMATH

Very soon after the eventful experiences at Lake Placid, Wendell was accepted into the dental school at the University of Missouri, Kansas City, Missouri. He was married in December 1945 to Donna MacKay, a good-looking blond student from Salt Lake City. His brother Sheridan had introduced her after he returned to the University of Utah. He began his dental training, financed by the GI Bill, in February 1946.

Wendell had been a fairly good student during his pre-war university experience but the three year-round accelerated dental program in Kansas City was not easy. His attitude was quite unpredictable, sometimes offensive. Additional difficulties surfaced during school when he suffered Malaria attacks every day after lunch. At first the classes were disrupted by the chills and fever, which were later ignored and accepted. Years later, he was told by the dental school dean that as a faculty they had been instructed he was not to fail his classes no matter what kind of behavioral or health-related problems were encountered. Being the only XPOW in the class had its perks.

There were those instructors who took an immediate dislike to him and to his unconventional behavior. Perhaps they felt some fearful apprehension as well. But they, too, had received the same instructions about not failing him. They were probably justified in making his success more difficult to achieve. He knew this and in retrospect he believed the additional challenges gave him the incentive to work a lot harder even though at the time he was angry about it. And he definitely did not enjoy it.

Through his own admission, his short-tempered testy attitude made life very difficult at times for his young wife. But she persevered because they had quickly become the parents of two beautiful little daughters along with the fact that she had no money with which to leave him and go home to Utah.

Soon after graduation in 1949 and his return to Utah, he was ready to set up practice but he had no money and no credit, just his dental degree coupled with the determination to work hard to provide for his family.

He eventually chose to practice in Manti, a small town in central Utah. Within a matter of weeks after he had made his decision, he found he was not able to borrow any money from a financial institution to set up an office. However, in a conversation with a salesman from a dental supply house, he was relieved to find the company would finance his equipment. He paid for it as his practice grew.

The twenty-two years after he was liberated from prison camp passed rapidly. Had it not been for the nightmares which continued to disrupt his sleeping hours, life would have been good. His practice was flourishing and his family had increased to four with the birth of a son and a third daughter. For the most part he was happy to be living and working in a rural area of his prison camp dreams. He and Don Tibbs, his attorney friend, built an office building together in downtown Manti. They also constructed their homes side by side and lived for thirty-five years in the best neighborhood in the world.

Besides the persistent reoccurring nightmares, there was a happening in Wendell's life which was repeated on an annual basis for several years after moving to Manti. February 5th marked the anniversary of his liberation from prison camp, and each year as the date neared, he became very restless and irritable. His solution to the problem was to pack a small bag, buy a bottle of booze, and head for an overnight stay in a Salt Lake hotel. After a day or two of being alone while he consumed the liquor and spent the time to resolve his feelings, he was able to return to his practice and to normal day-to-day living. There were few explanations for his actions and no apologies.

Quite by accident, he ran into an old friend who was a clinical psychologist. He told this friend of the nagging disruptive nightmares he was still experiencing and was surprised at the simple solution offered. He was told he needed to go back to the Philippine prison camp sites and take his wife with him. For a while the nightmares would reoccur, but she would also be in them. In the recesses of his cognitive processes, he knew that she was not present when he was a prisoner and eventually the dreams would no longer manifest themselves.

Finding it almost too easy to believe it would work, and the fact that a trip to the Islands was very expensive, the advice was ignored for several months. Finally, in May of 1967, the McGarrys borrowed the money to finance the trip and they were off to Manila.

Within a period of a few weeks after returning home, the nightmares ceased to plague him. Occasionally they would return after seeing a wartime movie or indulging in discussions where he was questioned about his experiences. Then his sleeping time would be short and troubled, sometimes a matter of three or four hours. Normally he never slept more than six hours a night. Oddly enough, the need for the annual solitary February sojourn to Salt Lake City disappeared about the same time as the nightmares.

Many times Wendell lamented the fact that the VA had not provided any kind of mental health assistance to the POWs of WWII. There had been excellent physical care in the military hospitals as well as an abundance of written material pertaining to the GI Educational and other benefits. But the tremendous need for mental help for the symptomatic Post Traumatic Stress Disorder simply was not there.

We saw graphic evidence of this demonstrated in the behavior of several XPOWs with whom we traveled to the Philippines in the spring of 1982. Thirty-seven years after the war's termination, hate and bitterness for the enemy still dominated their lives. They were miserable human beings who drank too much and spoke in terms of severe retribution. They were a source of deep concern and pity for the rest of the XPOWs who had adjusted to post-war society and were living good, productive lives.

The most important thing in the minds of Wendell's young grandchildren about Grandpa's time in prison camp was that he had very nearly starved to death. At each mealtime it was the theme at the table, "Clean your plate and don't waste any food, because Grandpa didn't have much when he was in prison camp." No matter what was served, no one took any more of it than they could eat. Nothing was to be left on the plate and wasted. It was firmly ingrained into the minds of all of them. Even now these phrases can be heard repeated in their homes to great-grandchildren.

Very soon after moving to Manti, Wendell became deeply involved in the workings of the community. He practiced family dentistry for thirty-five years where he assisted countless patients in raising their families while supplying excellent dental care, often without compensation. He was active in the Utah Dental Association and served as Chairman of the Utah State Board of Dental Examiners. He attended the 1945 dental class reunions at UMKC on an annual basis and he kept in close touch with many of his classmates.

For more than fifty years he was a member of the Manti American Legion Post Thirty-One and a past Commander. While serving on the Utah State Board of Directors of the Veterans of Foreign Wars he was instrumental in obtaining funding and building of the Utah Veteran's Cemetery. He was a former Commander of the Northwest Chapter of the American Defenders of Bataan (ADBC) and Corregidor as well as a member of the National Chapter of ADBC. He learned to love and respect those POWs and cherish their mutual friendship.

He served as War Bond Chairman and as Chairman of the local Draft Board for twenty years. As an avid Republican he served as Sanpete County Chairman. He never missed an opportunity to vote.

He was on the Utah State Judicial Board and a Board Member on the Gunnison Utah Correctional Facility. He served for seventeen years on the State of Utah Board of Parks and Recreation where he acted for seven years as Chairman. For many years he was a Citizen Board Member of the National Recreation and Parks Board and in 1990 he received their coveted State Service Award. Many of these positions were done concurrently.

He was active in the Lion's Club where he was elected as District Governor of the Southern Utah District. He was a Sanpete County Commissioner and a member of the Ephraim, Utah Library Board. In later years he was an active member of the LDS church as well.

Friends were very much a part of Wendell's life. He kept in touch with high school friends, dental school buddies, XPOW friends and those with whom he served in state government agencies via Christmas cards, letters, phone calls, and visits. His Manti friends were on the top of his list. He loved having dinner with them and he looked forward each winter to a seaside-on-the-beach vacation with them.

Amazing as it was, his ample public service record continued well into his retirement at the age of sixty-two. He was also a devoted husband, (thirty-five years with his first wife who passed away in 1979, and twenty-four years with his second). Father of nine children, five of them step children, grandfather to forty-three, and great grandfather to thirty-two, he played with his family and provided well for them. He taught them to work, to love their country, to respect and love their God, and to love each other.

Wendell was an animal lover. He always had a dog or a cat to follow him around as he tended his garden. They were his special friends.

He spent a good deal of time playing solitaire and was always good for a game of gin rummy, which he usually won. He loved teaching his small grandchildren to read numbers as they played "Go Fish." Sincerely believing that none of his college-age grandchildren should go away to a university without a comprehensive knowledge of poker, he supplied ten dollar rolls of quarters and he taught them. Their losses were returned when they were ready to drive back to school. Gas cost money.

He was an avid reader, particularly during his sleepless nocturnal hours or when he was a passenger on an aircraft. He was a master gardener, generously sharing his bounteous harvest. He tenderly nurtured fragrant Peace roses and shared them with neighbor ladies. He played golf—lots of golf. He and his wife traveled worldwide.

He loved buying jewelry when they traveled and especially enjoyed acquiring pieces made by Native Americans who lived in Southern Utah. He bought rings, bracelets, and necklaces by the dozens for his wife, daughters, and granddaughters whenever he visited State Parks.

Wendell never even considered the remote possibility he might be a hero, but he was in every sense of the word. Along with thousands of other young Americans, he put his life on hold, literally for years, to answer his country's call to arms. In doing what he did, when it needed to be done, he suffered physical torture and mental pain, but in the process he learned. He became endowed with supreme patience and self control. Through his understanding of others when he perceived hurt, sorrow, and loss in their lives, he saw their needs and he did his best to fill the void.

He was generous with his time and resources, giving and sharing with those who were less fortunate. His motto was:

> If you don't leave this world a better place than it was when you came into it you haven't done your job!

Bravo, my darling husband, you have done your work well!

Gwen J. McGarry

PHOTO ACKNOWLEDGMENTS

My love and thanks to daughter Nancee McGarry Ott who shared the 1960 photo of her dad, Dr. Wendell H. McGarry, and mother, Donna Mackay McGarry. Kay Boulter, State Park Photographer, has my special thanks for his photo of Wendell and Gwen at Palisade State Park Golf Course, Sterling, Utah in 1981. For family pictures of Wendell's parents and siblings as well as the priceless picture of him and his smiling mother arriving at the Salt Lake Airport March 26, 1945, my sincere love and appreciation to his 92 year old sister LaRue McGarry Brewster. Photos of Corregidor Museum photos taken in 2006 on my last trip to the Philippines: Corregidor Island, Colonel Jesus Villamore Filipino Flying Ace, General George Moore, Philippine President and Mrs. Quezon with their family while at the Malinta Tunnel. Photo of the Manila Hotel Lobby from a postcard Wendell purchased in 1981. All other Philippine Island pictures I took on trips to the islands in 1982, 1998 and 2006. To our very dear friend, renowned Montana artist and former POW Ben Steele, my undying love and gratitude for his POW drawing at Cabanatuan Prison. Newspaper clippings from the *Salt Lake Tribune*. Photo of "Joyce" found in one of her letters to Wendell.

My very special thanks to all of you who so generously contributed time and effort in looking up sixty year-old photos as well as more recent ones; putting faces with names appearing in the book.

WORKS CITED

"Adventure 5." [Brochure for Pearl Harbor Cruise.] N.p.: n.p.,n.d.

Aluit, Alfonzo J. "Corregidor." *Galleon Guide Book*. Caloocan City: Zone Printing Co. 1980.

Garrett, George, Mrs. [Report.] *Prisoner of War Bulletin* 2.1 (January 1944):3.

Jacobsen, Gene. Personal interview. January 2003.

McGarry, Wendell H. Letter to Fern McGarry. April 19, 1941.

---. Letter to Fern McGarry. April 26, l941.

---. Letter to Fern McGarry. May 10, 1941.

---. Letter to Fern McGarry. May 21, 1942.

---. Talk. Manti High School, Manti, Utah. November 11, 1993.

---. Talk. May 26, 1997.

---. Talk. Senior Citizens. Ephraim, Utah. May 30, 1994.

Villa, Sol L. "The Fall." *Chronicle Magazine* n.d.: 7.

CPSIA information can be obtained at www.ICGtesting.com
Printed in the USA
BVOW11s0527170714

359478BV00008B/14/P